YEOVIL
IN THE SECOND
WORLD WAR

YEOVIL

IN THE SECOND WORLD WAR

JACK SWEET

FONTHILL

Fonthill Media Language Policy

Fonthill Media publishes in the international English language market. One language edition is published worldwide. As there are minor differences in spelling and presentation, especially with regard to American English and British English, a policy is necessary to define which form of English to use. The Fonthill Policy is to use the form of English native to the author. Jack Sweet was born and educated in Yeovil, Somerset; therefore, British English has been adopted in this publication.

Fonthill Media Limited
Fonthill Media LLC
www.fonthillmedia.com
office@fonthillmedia.com

First published in the United Kingdom and the United States of America 2020

British Library Cataloguing in Publication Data:
A catalogue record for this book is available from the British Library

Typeset in 10.5pt on 13pt Sabon
Printed and bound in England

Acknowledgements

My great appreciation and thanks to the editor of the *Western Gazette*, for permission to use articles from the *Gazette* in this book. The photograph of the bomb-damaged houses in Gordon Road is reproduced with the permission of the National Archives reference HO192/875.

Once again, a special thank you to Margaret, my wife, for her continuing patience and tolerance during my many writing adventures.

Every effort has been made to contact copyright holders. In the unlikely event that you have been overlooked, please get in touch so the appropriate credit can be included in future editions.

Contents

Introduction

The armistice that ended the fighting on the Western Front on 11 November 1918 was not the official end of the First World War; it was not until the peace treaty was signed at Versailles in France on 28 June 1919 that the war was finally declared to be over.

Great Britain and the empire declared Saturday, 19 July 1919 to be Peace Day, and on that day in Yeovil, following a service of thanksgiving held in the open on Wyndham Fields, nearly 1,000 veterans and war widows marched through the town in the rain to a civic welcome and luncheon in one of the large hangars at the Westland Aircraft Works.

No one marching on that wet Saturday in the summer of 1919 could have dreamt in their wildest nightmares that twenty years later, the nation would be at war with Nazi Germany.

The First World War was followed by worldwide political, economic, and social turmoil, which saw the rise of fascism in Italy under Mussolini, Nazism in Germany under Hitler, communism in Russia under Stalin, and the ambitions of Imperial Japan in the Far East.

The history of the Second World War (which broke out in September 1939 and ended with the surrender of Japan in August 1945) has been, and no doubt will continue to be, the source of thousands of books, articles, and millions of words together with thousands of films, TV shows, and radio programmes.

Yeovil in the Second World War is not a history of the conflict, and it is not even an attempt to write one; it is a personal look back to the life of my hometown during those six momentous years and includes some of the articles I contributed to the *Western Gazette*; they are also the years during which I grew up.

Our Fight for Freedom

In 1948, the *Western Gazette* published a twenty-page booklet under the title of *YEOVIL 1939–1945 Seen through journalist eyes*. Following an introduction by the mayor, Alderman Ben Dening, came the following article written by Mr R. G. Kemble (the *Western Gazette*'s sports editor) that, I believe, sets the scene for the articles presented in the following pages, which, in turn, might go some way to recording Yeovil's story in the Second World War.

Our Fight for Freedom

This simple story of the common people who fought for freedom could be told of towns and cities throughout the length and breadth of this land of ours, but for us, the people of Yeovil, it has a significance of its own—it is the contribution we made during those perilous years of war.

To the four corners of the earth went Yeovil's fighting sons to serve on land, on sea and in the air. As did their fathers in that 'war to end all wars' a generation before, many found a grave in the ocean or under foreign soil. To those worthy sons of a proud Borough who went carefree into battle and to those at home, playing no less a share in final victory who were struck down by a death which rained from the skies, this story is dedicated.

From those never-to-be-forgotten days after Dunkirk when remnants of the shattered but gallant British Expeditionary Force rested in summer weather in Yeovil gardens and on Yeovil pavements, and when the very night itself vibrated with the rumble of trains bearing the broken and maimed to hospital, until that day of their return when D-Day revealed the greatest armada the world has ever known, Yeovil saw more than a mere glimpse of each changing tide of six years of war.

The story opened in fact two days before that ill-fated Sunday of September in 1939, when the Prime Minister told a waiting nation that we were at war ... evacuees, the first of thousands that were to come to the district, found sanctuary, hospitality and education in the town. As they day by day grew older in our midst, they saw something of the endeavour and sacrifice made by the people who sheltered them.

At factory benches, office desks and in shops, filling the places of the Borough's sons and daughters who joined the ranks of the armed forces, were the old people, renewed after retirement, mothers of children and teen-age youngsters.

There was no campaign or theatre of war in which men from this town did not serve. They came back from the hell that was Dunkirk, returning with the invasion forces to sweep through to devastated Berlin. They knew too, the heat of the day and the cold of the night in the desert warfare of North Africa; while fighting disease as well as a relentless enemy they served with the 'Forgotten Army' in the steaming jungles of Burma.

None perhaps knew the rigours of war more than those who served with the Royal Navy and the Merchant Navy. From the action in the mouth of the Plate to the final surrender of the Japs in Tokyo Bay was a chapter of valour and stoicism. In the air Yeovil men were numbered among the gallant 'Few' to whom this country owes so much and with the changing fortunes of battle they were at the controls and in the gun turrets of the heavy bombers which brought Germany cringing to her knees. Many there were who knew not the victory of arms. They were the men behind the barbed-wire enclosures of prison camps in Europe and the Far East, awaiting seemingly endless years for the day of liberation.

What of those men and women who, of necessity remained at home? On an evening in May when the day was bright as the news was dark, the Secretary of State for War came to the microphone and called all men between the ages of 17 and 65 who were not already serving in the forces to join the Local Defence Volunteers. As did they rally to the call of Kitchener in the first world war, so did they in that darkening hour answer the bidding of Mr. Anthony Eden. And the Home Guard was born.

In terms of money the borough's contribution in savings to the national effort was £5,000,000. Aid to the Red Cross Society, Prisoners of War Fund, Russia and China was given. Nearly £2000 was subscribed to the Mayor's Gift Fund to provide Christmas gifts for Yeovilians serving in all parts of the world. Those abroad received 500 cigarettes and then there was £5 each for the prisoners of war.

Yeovil still bears the scars from the ten times that the town suffered from enemy action. In all forty-nine people were killed or died of injuries—five children were among them—and a further 122 were injured.

A third of the Borough's houses were damaged-while sixty-eight were totally destroyed. Yeovil's first experience of bombing on October 7th and 8th, 1940 was the most serious. On the first occasion high explosives destroyed and damaged property, including Burton's in Middle Street, the Methodist Church in Vicarage Street and dwellings in Grove Avenue, Summerleaze Park and Kingston Estate. On the following day Preston Grove suffered badly. Twenty-seven people were killed in these two raids. Two of the bombs made direct hits on shelters, one in Preston Grove and the other in the Methodist Church.

In the last raid on August 5th 1942, when two 'hit and run' Focke Wolfe [*sic*.] fighter bombers sneaked over the town just before dusk, nearly a thousand houses were damaged at Grass Royal, Dampier Street and Gordon Road. The 500kg bombs with a few seconds delayed-action were dropped from a low altitude and one of them, after hitting the ground, bounced a distance of 250 yards clearing a number of dwellings before landing and exploding in Dampier Street.

The attacks on the town varied from formations of twenty machines to 'hit and run' raids by one or two fighter bombers, single aircraft on special missions and bombs dropped from isolated machines as they tried to escape interception by our own fighter aircraft. Although the Westland Aircraft works was undoubtedly an enemy target it was hit only once, and then the damage was only slight. The attack carried out in daylight by a single aircraft resulted in damage and fatal casualties when bombs were dropped on houses outside the target area.

Men and girls of the Royal Observer Corps and the Air Raid Precaution services, in which three thousand personnel were involved, responded splendidly. When danger materialised the zeal and efficiency of the wardens, heavy rescue and Voluntary Aid Detachments, and other services came fully up to expectations and the Women's Voluntary

Services were on hand at all hours with refreshments. Their most exacting period was during 1940 and 1941 when day and night alerts kept them on duty for hours at a time. Altogether there were nearly 400 alerts.

The burden borne by the Invasion Committee, the Police and Special Constabulary was heavy.

Like the National Fire Service, first-aid and rescue parties were sent to reinforce the heavily raided towns of Bristol, Exeter and Weston-Super-Mare. Help was given to London during the worst period of the flying-bomb attacks.

The Last Pre-war Christmas

It was a white Christmas in 1938, the first in Yeovil for more than ten years. The cold weather started during the week before Christmas with severe frosts and snow and lasted until Boxing Day when temperatures at last began to rise; by New Year, it was like early spring.

For some Yeovilians, Christmas would not be a very happy one. There was quite a bit of unemployment worsened by the effects of the weather on the local building and construction industry. Over 400 people received assistance by grocery vouchers, food parcels, and joints of meat or coal from the mayor's Christmas fund in partnership with the Yeovil United Charities. Thirty-four full joints of beef were distributed by the Yeovil and District Trades Council and toys given by Woolworths were taken by the mayoress to children in their homes. Joints of meat were distributed from the Corn Exchange, and the Girl Guides assisted in delivering gifts to needy families in the town.

However, trade was brisk in Yeovil and Christmas Eve saw the shops full of last-minute shoppers and townspeople taking in the atmosphere of the lights, decorations, and the general good feeling of the season made more festive by the covering of snow and sparkling frost.

There was disappointment for the patients in the district hospital when a case of the very infectious and dangerous scarlet fever was diagnosed, and the wards were closed to Christmas Day visitors. The staff, however, did their best to cheer up their charges by decorating the wards, providing a large Christmas tree; also, Santa Claus arrived for the children. There was a turkey dinner, Christmas pudding, cakes, fruit, chocolate, sweets, and crackers and toys for the young patients, all of which went some way to make up for the absence of family and friends on Christmas Day.

The 'inmates' of the Preston Close public assistance institution (Summerlands), which in an earlier time had been called the workhouse, were reported to have enjoyed a 'happy time'. The dining hall, entrance hall, and wards were hung with blue and yellow decorations and there was a special breakfast and dinner on Christmas Day when the nurses toured the wards singing carols and Christmas hymns. There was a heavy post of parcels, letters, and cards, and no inmate was overlooked. On Boxing Day, the special Christmas tea was followed by a concert given by the institution staff and inmates. The bedridden patients were able to enjoy the programme, which was 'broadcast in the hospital wards by means of amplification equipment'.

Each of the nineteen children in the Preston Park House Children's Home received a present and a greetings card on Christmas morning; more presents were distributed by Father Christmas at the Boxing Day party around a giant Christmas tree.

A tree given by Alderman W. Earle Tucker festooned with coloured lights was set up in St John's Church, and nearly 300 people attended the Christmas Communion. As Christmas Day fell on a Sunday, the town's churches and chapels combined their Christmas and Sunday services. Collections of money and goods were taken to assist the work of relieving hardship in distressed areas of South Wales and other parts of the country. At Holy Trinity, the Sunday before Christmas was 'Christmas Tree Sunday' when the parents of the Sunday school children and members of the congregation brought gifts to the tree set up in the church. There was a generous response and the toys were sent to the vicar's former parish of Bethnal Green in London for distribution to poor children at a New Year's Day party.

Despite the weather and the unemployment in the Yeovil area, the post office recorded a 10 per cent increase in traffic over 1937; greetings telegrams rose by 50 per cent. Eighty temporary postmen were employed in the town and all mail was cleared daily on time from the head post office.

Showing at the Odeon cinema was the *Private Life of Henry VIII* with Charles Laughton and *I've Got a Horse* starring Sandy Powell; *Mr Moto's Gamble* featuring Peter Lore and *The Adventures of Marco Polo* with Gary Cooper, completed the Gaumont Palace Christmas Programme; and the Central cinema in Church Street presented *There's Always a Woman* and *Stepping Toes*.

However, as Yeovil was enjoying the festival of Christmas, the war clouds were gathering elsewhere in the world; in his Christmas message in the *Yeovil Review*, the Rev. F. Buffard, minister of South Street Baptist Church, wrote:

> What a Christmas! Bombs raining down on Chinese Towns, Spaniards at one another's throats, Arabs and Jews at daggers drawn, Europe teeming with refugees, the air darkened with hatred and fear, and millions without work for hand or mind … learn from Christmas how to love when the festival is over. So let us resolve that we will act on December 25th with generosity, with thoughtfulness and forgiveness in our hearts for all. There is enough resource in Jesus Christ to turn every day into a Christmas Day.

Christmas 1938 would be the last peacetime festive season. Christmas 1939 would see the nation at war for the next six years, and things would never be the same again.

1939

Some Important Events

1 September	Germany invades Poland.
3 September	Great Britain and France declare war on Germany.
27 September	Poles surrender at Warsaw.
September	British Expeditionary Force lands in France and assembles along the Belgian/French border. During the coming winter and spring, there is little combat and the period is called the 'Phoney War'; the Battle of the Atlantic begins against the German U-Boats attacking naval convoys; civilian petrol use controlled.

The Beginning of Houndstone and Lufton Camps

War clouds were gathering rapidly over Europe in the spring of 1939, when the government introduced the conscription of young men between twenty and twenty-one years of age into the militia for six months training to be followed by three and a half years of service in the Territorial Army or Special Army Reserve. Some 300,000 militiamen would be called-up during the summer of 1939, and the government began an urgent search for sites for training camps. On 19 May 1939, the *Western Gazette* reported that the War Office had compulsorily purchased the 196 acres of Houndstone Farm on the western outskirts of Yeovil for two military training camps to accommodate 2,500 militiamen and contractors were already on site; completion of the huts and associated services was scheduled for 15 July.

The construction of the camps was under the direction of the Royal Engineers with Messrs John Mowlem & Co. as main contractors, and the urgent recruitment began for some 200 carpenters and 1,000 labourers required to build the hundreds of wooden huts and provide the services within the timescale of two months.

On 2 June, the *Gazette* informed readers that work was well underway, with several hundred men already on site and living in tents. Two weeks later, the newspaper reported that although the work was progressing satisfactorily, the grave shortage of skilled carpenters was causing concern; it went on to explain:

Four hundred men are now employed as labourers digging the foundations of the hundred or so wooden huts to house the 2,500 of Britain's first militiamen. They are aided by strange-looking mechanical excavators and where once was green pasture, land is now an apparent mass of deep trenches in which men labour waist high, and huge amounts of clay soil.

The foundations of the 1,000-seater cinema had been laid, the camps' electricity supply was already provided, a water service was laid on from Odcombe, and the drainage system was being linked to the town's sewers in Preston Road.

A week later, on 23 June, the *Western Gazette* reported that over 1,000 men were now employed on the site, with more pouring into Yeovil every day. A national recruiting drive had supplied the skilled carpenters, and completion of 400 huts, the parade ground, cinema, sports pitches, recreation, mess buildings, churches, and chapels by 15 July was still anticipated.

A small tented town with two canteens was home to the workforce, and the outpatients' department at Yeovil hospital was being kept busy treating many of the minor accidents suffered by the men during their twelve-hour hour day.

The demand for skilled tradesmen and labourers was, however, causing problems in the local building industry, especially from the higher wages being paid on the camp sites. Mr L. S. Kibby, the contractor for the Yeovil borough council's St Michael's Avenue housing scheme, had lost some sixty men from his workforce of 130, and the work was now several weeks behind time. Messrs F. R. Bartlett Ltd had lost ten, Messrs Montacute and Riggs stated that their contracts were in trouble, and fourteen men had left Messrs Lucas Bros. It was also reported that many agricultural workers had left their farms for the high wages at Houndstone and Lufton camps.

The first draft of regular soldiers arrived during the last week of June, but on Tuesday 12 July, some 500 workers went on unofficial strike. Sixty plumbers were the first to down tools, complaining that the operator of a pipe screwing machine was not a plumber and was earning only six pence an hour less than the skilled tradesmen. A few hours later, 200 carpenters, painters, and mechanics, together with a like number of labourers, struck following the dismissal of a chargehand, but both disputes were soon settled, and the men returned to work two days later.

On Saturday 16 July, the first batch of militiamen arrived, and during the next few days, the number increased to over 2,000. However, the permanent camp had not been completed on time, and for several months, many of the conscripts would enjoy the luxury of army tents. The young men were welcomed to their new home by heavy rain followed by several weeks of very unsettled weather, but the *Western Gazette* would report that 'The men have maintained the cheerful demeanour with which from the time they set foot in Yeovil they have faced the prospects of the new life'.

The work was completed later in the year, and the camps would be enlarged during the war years to come. Houndstone and Lufton camps would not only become an important part in the life of Yeovil and the surrounding district for over thirty years, but also in the lives of the thousands of British and United States servicemen and women who passed through their gates.

The Co-operative Society's Golden Jubilee Fete

In the summer of 1889, the Yeovil and District Co-operative Society opened its first shop in Middle Street, and in June 1939, the society celebrated its fiftieth anniversary. The main event of the golden jubilee week was a carnival in aid of the Yeovil Hospital; the celebrations began with the election of the carnival queen by the audience of the Odeon cinema during the Saturday evening performance on 10 June. Miss Phyllis Swaffield was elected queen and Joan Webb, Joan King, and Ursula Smith were voted her attendants.

Saturday 17 June was the big day, and in the afternoon, the carnival procession assembled in the Park, while in the Borough, the carnival queen was crowned by the deputy mayor, Alderman S. C. Clothier. When all was ready, the procession of twenty-four floats and over 100 walking entries set out for the Huish football ground to the accompaniment of the Sherborne Boys' Brigade and the Bridgwater Imperial Bands. The 'Royal' float was decorated with palms and flowers, and the queen sat with her three attendants under a blue canopy.

Reporting on the procession, the *Western Gazette* noted:

Among the most striking tableaux were those entered by the departments of the society. 'Dr. Ike and his Divi Kids' was a diverting skit by the Bakery Dept on Will Hay and his 'scholars'. Of feminine interest was the Drapery Dept.'s display of beach wear against a background of blue sea and yellow sands. An 'armoured' car symbolising milk as a national defence against disease was surmounted by a huge bottle of milk and was entered by the Co-operative Dairy Dept., whilst the Confectionery Dept. produced a tempting array of delicacies, including a jubilee cake. The Furnishing Dept. exhibited a tastefully furnished drawing room. Turbaned natives who defied the cold for the sake of realism and an English tea planter figured in a plantation scene by the Central Grocery Dept. A reminder of the movement's work for youth was given by Miss Holland and the Misses A. Norris, O. Sutton, J. Voaden and E. Butt, in an attractive tableaux [*sic*.] depicting the call of the open air.

The local branch of the Amalgamated Engineering Union presented a tableau of 'The Tolpuddle Martyrs', and the National Union of Glovers displayed the several processes in glove-making. The machine girls of the Stoke-Sub-Hamdon glove-makers Messrs J. H. Walters Ltd presented 'By a Dutch Mill', and Miss Irene Spurrett's pupils contributed 'Snow White and the Seven Dwarfs'. Mrs Cowles's 'keep fit' class appeared in 'Bonnie Scotland', and Mrs R. Ostler's presentation of 'The Band Waggoners' drew cheers as spectators recognised 'Arthur Askey', 'Stinker Murdoch', and 'Syd White' from the popular radio show. The *Western Gazette* described the entry of the staff of Messrs Aplin and Barrett of St. Ivel Cheese fame as 'an attractive beach scene', while the Hospital Savings Association presented what else but a hospital scene. The *Gazette* recorded that 'Consuming cider, bread and cheese and onions, Mr E. Hewlett's party gave the only rural touch in "The Last Load"'.

The two best entries in the walking groups were Miss Irene Spurrett's pupils as 'Toy Soldiers' and Mr Leslie's skit 'The Conscripts' (only a few months earlier, as war clouds gathered over Europe, conscription had been introduced for the armed forces).

Prizes for the best tableaux and walking entries were presented at the Huish football ground by the wife of the Yeovil Society's general manager.

During the Saturday evening, a mass meeting held in the Huish ground was addressed by Mr Herbert Morrison, MP (grandfather of Lord Peter Mandelson), who earlier had been introduced to the carnival queen and her attendants.

Jubilee week ended with a fireworks display described as 'one of the best seen in Yeovil', and among the set pieces, 'The Shipwreck' and 'The Launching of the Lifeboat' were said to have been especially attractive.

No one enjoying those fireworks in that June evening of 1939 could have imagined that within three months, the Second World War would have broken out.

Westland Aircraft, 1939

The story of Westland Aircraft (now Leonardo), from its beginnings over a century ago in 1915, has been thoroughly covered by a number of authors over the years, including the years of the Second World War from 1939 to 1945, but any book remembering Yeovil during that conflict must include an account, no matter how brief, of the company during those momentous years.

On the outbreak of war in September 1939, Westland Aircraft was building the company's Westland Lysander, their most successful aircraft to see operational service during the conflict. The Lysander (or 'Lizzie') would see service in a number of roles, including army co-operation, reconnaissance, air-sea rescue, and the aircraft's best-known role in working with RAF Special Duty squadrons communicating with resistance movements in Nazi-occupied Europe, supplying arms and equipment, delivering and picking up secret agents, and rescuing downed Allied airmen. During its operational history, Lysanders served also with a number of Allied air forces; by the end of the war, over 1,600 Lysanders had been built.

Another Westland-designed aircraft was the twin-engined, cannon-armed, single-seat Westland Whirlwind, which, despite being found unsuitable in the role of a fighter, was an excellent fighter-bomber during the early years of the war due to the heavy firepower of its nose-mounted cannon. However, only 116 Whirlwinds were built and saw active service with two RAF squadrons.

To combat the possible threat of very high altitude bombing by the Luftwaffe, Westland Aircraft developed the Westland Welkin, but as the threat did not materialise, the aircraft never entered operational service; even so, seventy-seven were built.

During the war, in addition to building Lysanders and Whirlwinds, Westland Aircraft constructed some 2,500 Spitfires and Seafires as well as modifying US-manufactured Mohawks, Tomahawks, and Kittyhawks.

The German Luftwaffe was well aware of Westland Aircraft and carried out ten bombing attacks from 1940 to 1942 with the Yeovil factory as their target. Of the bombs that rained down on the town, only two hit their target; despite the tragic deaths of four employees, the damage caused did not affect aircraft production. The stories of the bombing raids are related later in this book.

Due to the threat of air attack, Westland dispersed some of its operations to other parts of Yeovil and the surrounding district. Workshops for the manufacture of small parts were established underneath Messrs Vincent's pre-war car park behind the former Odeon cinema in Court Ash; Petter's old Nautilus Works at Reckleford was used for storage of sheet metal and other equipment; and perishable raw materials and rubber were stored in buildings now forming part of the Abbey Manor Trading Estate, off Stourton Way.

Over the past 100 years, Westland Aircraft has become inextricably linked with the life of Yeovil, both socially and industrially and the following authors and their books well document the Westland story: *Westland Aircraft Since 1915* (Putnam, 1991), *Westland: The Archive Photographs Series* (Chalfont, 1997), and *Westland: A History* (Tempus, 2002) by D. N. James; *Quiet Country Town: A celebration of 100 Years of Westland at Yeovil* (The History Press, 2015) by D. A. Gibbings; *Westland 50* (Ian Allen, 1965) by W. Taylor and M. F. Allward; and *British Aviation* by H. Penrose.

RNAS Yeovilton—HMS *Heron*

As Westland Aircraft (Leonardo) has become an important part of the life of Yeovil over the past 100 years, so has Royal Naval Air Station (RNAS) Yeovilton—HMS *Heron* since 1939.

On 1 April 1918, the Royal Flying Corps and the Royal Naval Air Service (the flying arm of the Royal Navy) merged to form the Royal Air Force. In 1924, the Fleet Air Arm was established as an organisational unit of the RAF, operating aircraft on serving naval warships, but in 1937, naval aviation was transferred back to the Royal Navy.

As war clouds were gathering in 1938, the Admiralty began to urgently look for new airfields to provide training facilities for the government's programme for new aircraft and aircraft carriers. In July 1939, the Admiralty commandeered 417 acres of farmland and work began almost immediately on constructing the new Royal Naval Air Station, which would bear the name of Yeovilton, its village neighbour to the south.

Early in 1940, Westland Aircraft established a sub-factory in the first hangar built on the airfield, and in June 1940, the site was commissioned as HMS *Heron*. The German Luftwaffe took an interest in the newly constructed airfield and bombed it on three occasions during the summer of 1940 and once again in 1941. The damage was slight; although five Westland employees were wounded when the company's hangar was hit, thankfully, no one was killed.

During the following war years, HMS *Heron* played a leading role in training naval airmen and forming squadrons for active service.

Since the end of the war in 1945, Yeovilton has expanded to over 1,000 acres of airfield, and at the time of writing (2019), the Royal Naval Air Station is the home of both the Royal Naval and Army Air Corps helicopter forces, the Royal Naval Historic Flight and the Royal Navy Fleet Air Arm Museum.

During the years of the Second World War, many Yeovilton pilots and aircrew were killed in training or on operational service from the airfield, and between 1940 and 1942, fifteen airmen killed in air accidents were buried in the churchyard of St. Bartholomew, Yeovilton. In 1942, a naval cemetery was opened on the southern boundary of the churchyard; in 1993, following the purchase of the church by the Royal Navy, St Bartholomew's became the Fleet Air Arm's Memorial church. housing the Fleet Air Arm's Roll of Honour and Memorial Chapel.

Yeovilton's story is well-told in the book published in 1990 by the Fleet Air Arm Museum to commemorate fifty years of RNAS Yeovilton: *YEOVILTON, The History of the Royal Naval Air Station, Yeovilton, 1940–1990* by Cdr P. M. Rippon, MSc, CEng, MIMechE, MRAeS, RN and Graham Mottram MA (Cantab), CEng.

The Blackout

On 3 September 1939, the day war broke out, regulations were brought in requiring streetlights to be switched off, and all householders had to curtain their windows to prevent any light being seen by enemy aircraft flying overhead. The *Yeovil Review* of September wrote:

> Just a week ago, Yeovil with its excellent shops, was ablaze with light. Cinemas were well patronised, village fetes and shows were being organised, football clubs were getting into stride, and summer sport and holidays were in full swing, Now all has changed.
>
> Yeovil is and must continue blacked out. Quite a number, in fact there are but few now, who will hear the command of the Special Constable on his nightly beat cry 'Put those lights out!' But there are still those few. Just a reminder, to those who think this fuss and nonsense is going a bit too far. The safety of the Town with all its thousands of women and children may be jeopardised by a stray light blazing in the sky, forgotten. Here is a phrase taken from the official notice concerning the 'Black Out'—'Any person who permits any glimmer of light to escape from his premises so that it can be seen from the outside constitutes a public danger, matches must not be struck in the open air. Any torches used in the open or in those portions of the premises not effectively screened should be properly screened with paper in the lens or a dark blue bulb.' Note—The penalty for offending in any way against the lighting restrictions is a fine of £50 [average weekly wage £5] or three months imprisonment.
>
> Special Constables have already reported insufficient and inadequate screening of household lights. It is not sufficient to draw the blind and switch on the electric light. Some streets are well and truly blacked out, at least they appear so from the front, but at the back the tell-tale glow through the drawn blinds betrays the presence of living accommodation. One must face the facts. It may be you who are placing the town in danger from enemy aircraft.
>
> Now, a word to the cyclist who before many weeks will find his ride home from work means travelling in the dark. You are not exempt from these lighting regulations. Front lights must be diffused by the use of paper if an electric light is used, and they are reminded that red rear lamps properly screened are now compulsory.
>
> Motorists, too have been warned. Temporary expedients for headlight screening must be dispensed with, side lamps, rear lamps, reversing and

'Stop' lamps must be reduced to their proper dimensions and lights diffused by the use of paper behind the lens. Travel by night will become increasingly more difficult. It will be better to keep the car in the garage at night than hazard a journey in the dark.

The first Yeovil blackout fatality was Mr Thomas Turner, a fifty-one-year-old painter employed at the new Houndstone army camp. He had been walking along Thorne Lane to the camp when he was knocked down and fatally injured by a lorry being driven with screened headlamps. In recording a verdict of 'Death by misadventure', the coroner suggested that pedestrians should wear something white to make themselves more visible during the present emergency.

By September 1944, the threat of German air raids had rapidly diminished, and the government allowed a 'Dim-Out' with street lighting equivalent to moonlight; however, if the air raid warnings sounded the full blackout was imposed. In April 1945, the blackout was abolished, and the streetlights went back on.

Evacuation

On Friday, 1 September 1939, the *Western Gazette* bore the headline 'REFUGEES FROM LONDON':

Since yesterday (Thursday) morning the authorities of Yeovil and district, who are responsible for the reception of refugees under the Government evacuation scheme have been working at top pressure to complete their arrangements for the billeting of the 11000 children and adults who will today (Friday) begin to arrive at Yeovil Town Station. The schemes had been prepared under the supervision of the Chief Billeting Officers, Major H.C.C. Batten, DSO. (Borough) and Mr C. A. Wilson (Rural).

Yeovil Borough is to receive 4,410, 2,207 being unaccompanied children and the remainder teachers, helpers and others, including mothers with children under school age. The first batch of about 630 children is expected at about 4.30 p.m. today (Friday) at the Town Station; and the appropriate times of other arrivals are 7.20 p.m. the same evening; the second day's 2 p.m. and 4.50 p.m.; the third day 2 p.m. and 7.20 p.m. Each train will contain 630. The parties will be marched to Messrs Aplin & Barrett's factory in Newton Road, and provided with liquid refreshments, either of cold milk or hot Ivelcon. They will then be taken to clearing stations—Grass Royal, Reckleford Infants, Huish Junior and Summerleaze Park Schools—where after registration they will be given 48 hours' emergency rations, and handed over to those who will take them to their billets.

Should it be found impossible to arrange for the billeting of any of the evacuees on the night of their arrival, they will be provided with temporary sleeping accommodation for the night in the Clearing Stations.

An appeal for lady volunteers to act as marshals was made by the chief billeting officer of Yeovil. Many of the enrolled volunteers were on holiday and although many had been communicated with by telegram, there would be a considerable shortage. Lady volunteers were asked to report to the Town Clerk's office.

During that Friday afternoon, some 1,350 London children arrived in four trains at Yeovil Town Station and were taken to the Liberal Club from where they were carried in buses and cars to surrounding villages. The first trainload of children destined for billets in Yeovil arrived forty minutes late at 5.30 p.m. and included a group of three-year-olds from a Blackfriar's nursery school and older children from Southwark and Camberwell. The youngsters were taken to Messrs Aplin and Barrett's nearby factory for their refreshments and where they were welcomed by the mayor, Alderman Beel, who with the onset of heavy thunderstorms ordered the requisition of buses to take them to the Clearing Stations.

Three hours later, the second train arrived with 425 children from two schools in the Elephant and Castle district, including thirty partially sighted youngsters. By now the difficulties of the volunteers in marshalling the young evacuees had been increased by the heavy rain and the 'blackout' order under which all street and public lights were turned off. The platforms at the Town Station were almost in total darkness and the volunteers were forced to sort the children into groups on the station forecourt in the dark and rain. It was long past midnight before most of the young evacuees were billeted and the few who could not be found accommodation stayed overnight in the schools. Two more trains arrived one after the other on Saturday bringing about 1,000 mothers and children, followed on Sunday 3 September, the day war was declared, by another 688 mothers and children.

The billeting officers and volunteers were presented with many problems in trying to accommodate whole families who had arrived unexpectedly with their children. One female evacuee was detained for some time by the officials as she could not give a satisfactory account of herself or explain which party she had come with. Some Greek women were unable to speak English, and none of the volunteers spoke Greek. However, despite the difficulties, by Sunday evening, all the evacuees had been found accommodation.

At the special meeting of the borough council on 4 September, the mayor paid tribute to the townspeople, officials, and volunteers for the welcome and hard work in receiving and billeting the evacuees under such difficult circumstances. Besides the large number of volunteers at the clearing centres, much good work had been carried by the Boy Scouts, Girl Guides, and Girls' Life Brigade, who acted as guides and messengers; many Girl Guides proved invaluable in looking after babies at the centres.

As many of the mothers with small children had been unable to bring their prams and pushchairs, an appeal was launched for these items together with an appeal for children's clothes.

For some reason, the author's parents did not have an evacuee, even though they were happy to have one and there was a room available, but there was a small boy billeted next door with Mr and Mrs Badland. The author remembers sitting with him in his mother's wicker washing basket pretending that it was a boat and singing 'Under the spreading chestnut tree, Mr Churchill said to me, "If you want to get your gas mask free, you must join the ARP"'.

The immediate large-scale bombing of London and the big cities did not occur as feared and some of the evacuees drifted back to their homes during the period of the 'phoney war', which lasted to the spring of 1940. However, many would return when the German bombing campaign began later in the year, and again in 1944, during the enemy's V-1 and V-2 attacks on the capital and the Home Counties.

In September 1939

Yeovil Football Week

In the last week of August 1939, and the last week of peace for six years, Yeovil and Petters United Football Club held a 'Yeovil Football Week' to help pay the £400 loss incurred during the 1938–39 season. The events included a 'Get Together Smoking Concert' and a 'Flannel Dance' in the Assembly Rooms, Princes Street. However, the highlight of the week was the Friday evening 'All Stars Variety Concert' in the Princes Theatre, featuring Crewkerne-born radio and film star Ralph Reader and members of his popular Gang Show, including Eric Christmas, George Cameron, Mac at the Piano, and the Twizzle Sisters. Also performing were the BBC singer soprano Doris Waller, the Pocock Brothers on piano and cornet, Paddy Ryan with his ukulele, and 'The Boy Step Dancer', Tony Mogg.

Identity Cards

The National Registration Bill being pushed through Parliament immediately following the outbreak of war had three main purposes: to support and facilitate any National Service arrangements; to provide up-to-date manpower and other population statistics to take the place of the 1931 census; and other incidental services such as the preservation of contact between members of families dispersed by evacuation, to facilitate proof of identity.

Everyone would be given an identity card after filling in a questionnaire that would be issued and collected in 65,000 districts and severe penalties would be introduced for breaking the provisions of the bill when it became law.

In the Churches

As soon as the outbreak of war was declared on Sunday morning (3 September), the evening services were brought forward to 6 p.m., so that the congregations could get home well before dark when it was feared the bombing would start. The fear of poison gas attack was also very great, and the *Western Gazette* reported that many of the congregation in St John's Church were carrying their gas masks to services.

Gas Masks for Under-Fives

By the day war broke, nearly everyone over the age of five years had been issued with a gas mask, but they would not be available for the under-fives. The reasoning was explained in the *Western Gazette* on 8 September:

Respirators for children under the age of five will not be issued in the No. 6 Area of Somerset at present. This is because of the children's relative freedom from danger in the unlikely event of the use of poison gas. Respirators are issued to adults for their use when it is essential for them to pass from place to place, at a time when they have been warned that the presence of poison gas in their neighbourhood is suspected. Young children will naturally be kept in the most suitable refuge room, where plans are carried out to make this room gas proof. In the unlikely event of this room becoming damaged, such children can be safely carried in a damp blanket, coat etc., to an alternative place of refuge.

However, following a great public outcry, by the following week, the *Gazette* reported:

Anti-gas helmets for babies are being produced as fast as the factories can make them and many thousands have already been issued to the most vulnerable areas. Supplies of respirators for small children are being treated on the same lines as babies' helmets.

Schools and Cinemas Close

As soon as war was declared on 3 September, all of Yeovil's schools were closed and the youngsters enjoyed a longer summer holiday. However, as the feared (and expected) Nazi bomber onslaught did not materialise, most everyday living resumed, and the schools went back on Monday 18 September.

Likewise, the town's three cinemas shut immediately, but they opened again within the week.

Everything in Readiness

The *Western Gazette* of 8 September 1939 reported:

With a few exceptions, Yeovil's defences are manned by voluntary service personnel. In the event of a 'raid' Yeovil's defence services would be quickly in action.

Hundreds of workers are giving up many hours of their spare time in order to do their National Service tasks, special constables, air raid wardens auxiliary firemen &c., taking their allocated hours of duty as a matter of course. This does not mean that Yeovil has all the volunteers required. The auxiliary fire service still requires men and in the east and north wards there is a serious shortage of wardens. At present there are 210 wardens in the borough, whereas the full complement is 240. Twenty-one warden posts have been manned day and night since the emergency arose, volunteers doing shifts of four hours in every twenty-four.

There are about 30 full-time firemen in the borough, consisting of A.F.S. volunteers and regular members of the brigade. Yeovil V.A.D.

Somerset/19 is now about 50 strong and first aid posts are being equipped at Preston Close, Hendford School (South Street), Poor Law Institute, Manor Hotel and Hendford Manor. Yeovil Chamber of Trade has decided that until further notice members of the Chamber should close their business premises at 6 p.m. on Monday, Tuesday and Wednesday, 1 p.m. on Thursday and 7 p.m. on Friday and Saturday [There was no Sunday opening in 1939].

Boy Scouts

All boy scouts in Yeovil were asked to wear their uniforms during the day 'To facilitate their identification when their services are required for messenger work etc.'

ARP Badges

The mayor of Yeovil, Alderman Frank Beel, presented air raid precaution (ARP) badges to thirty-three borough council workers who had passed a full anti-gas course. The men would form rescue and demolition teams and public services' rescue squads.

Ban on Sounding Hooters

An order was issued under defence regulations forbidding anyone to sound within public hearing a siren, hooter, whistle, rattle, bell, horn, or gong, except in accordance with directions for air raid warning purposes. However, the order did not apply to church bells or normal use of bicycle bells or motor horns.

A Blackout Casualty

Herbert Allot—who was employed by the Navy, Army, and Royal Air Force Institute (NAAFI) at the new Houndstone army camp—was knocked down by a car in the blackout on the Sunday evening that war was declared. He was taken to Yeovil hospital with a suspected fractured skull.

The Last Peacetime Coach Trips

On Sunday 3 September, local coach operators Barlow, Phillips & Co. had a full day excursion to Bournemouth, half-day to Weymouth, an afternoon mystery trip, and evening trips to West Bay. No doubt, there was much to talk about on those excursions.

4

1940

Some Important Events

January	One of the coldest on record.
9 April	End of 'Phoney War'; Germany invades Denmark and Norway.
10 May	*Blitzkrieg*—Germany invades Belgium, Holland, Luxembourg and France.
10 May	Prime Minister Neville Chamberlain resigns and is replaced by Winston Churchill.
26 May–4 June	Dunkirk evacuation of British and French troops.
14 June	German Army enters Paris.
22 June	France signs an armistice with Germany.
30 June	Germans occupy the Channel Islands, the only British territory to be occupied.
10 July–12 October	Battle of Britain.
7 September	The German air offensive against British industrial targets, cities, and towns begins: the Blitz.
17 September	Hitler postpones Operation Sea Lion, the invasion of Great Britain is never put into action.

Rationing begins in January with bacon, butter, and sugar (including sweets), followed by meat, jam, biscuits, breakfast cereals, cheese, eggs, lard, milk, and canned and dried fruit. Rationing in one form or another would continue for eight years following the end of the war (including bread from 1946 to 1948) with commodities being taken off the ration as post-war circumstances allowed. Rationing was finally abolished in July 1954 when meat rationing ended.

Defending the Home Front

In July 1939, the *Western Gazette* reported:

> Yeovil was reduced to ruins' in the recent Air Raid, when hundreds of members of the A.R.P. and other services came into action in the test of the town's defences that has yet to take place. As ambulances dashed down Middle Street with clanging bells, fire engines sped on their way to 'blazing' buildings, rescue parties and decontamination squads got busy, townspeople were given a glimpse of what might happen in a real raid. And amid all this havoc there was one bright spot of comedy to relieve the tension. One 'casualty' who thought he had been left lying in the wreckage of one of the main streets forgotten by the rescue squads, after waiting an hour, made a miraculous recovery and disappeared. When the rescue party for that locality arrived they found a note instead of a casualty. On it was written: 'Bled to Death— Gone Home'.

When the all-too-real war broke out less than two months later, the countrywide air raid precaution (ARP) services, established some two years before in response to the fear of widespread air attack, were mobilised.

Here in Yeovil, the ARP (renamed Civil Defence in 1941) was organised as follows:

Air raid wardens were given a variety of tasks, which included patrolling the streets of their locality to ensure compliance with the strict blackout regulations; ensuring that people found shelter during alerts and in air raids; assisting the police, fire, and rescue services when needed; and generally looking after their neighbourhoods. By 1943, there were 340 wardens based in twenty wardens' posts with their headquarters at Hendford Manor.

The fire guard (or fire watchers) would monitor and report the fall of incendiary bombs to the national fire service and were trained to tackle fires with their main weapon, the stirrup pump. The fire guard was comprised of street fire teams and guards at business premises controlled from its headquarters at Church house. Fire guard duty became compulsory in

1941 for all men between sixteen and sixty-three, and women aged twenty to forty. Some 6,000 Yeovil people were enrolled in the service by 1943.

Rescue parties were made up of sixty-two men in four teams; they were based at the borough council's depot off Vicarage Street.

Casualty services had a fixed first-aid post at Summerlands public assistance institution. There was only one doctor, who was assisted by eighty-six first aiders. The mobile first aid post at Yeovil Hospital had one doctor and twenty-nine first aiders.

First aid parties were made up from eight leaders along with sixty-three men and nine women first aiders. Three ambulances were driven and staffed by men of the Yeovil voluntary aid detachment Somerset, with nineteen based at the Salthouse Lane ambulance station.

The mortuary for the reception of fatal air raid casualties was at the old Lyde Lane isolation hospital. The superintendent was the town cemetery superintendent together with two voluntary assistants, a voluntary clerk, and ten council workmen 'available for duty'.

Mr H. A. C. Cooper, who lived at 97a Middle Street, was appointed to photograph unidentified fatal casualties brought to the mortuary. Three copies of each photograph would be made: one to be retained by the superintendent, the second sent to the local police, and the third to the town clerk.

Messengers were mainly teenagers on bicycles working with the various services.

Thankfully there were no poison gas attacks and the gas decontamination squad of twelve men was never needed but was kept in readiness.

Information came from the municipal offices, with its staff of twenty-six (including seven reserves). Thirteen places were designated as assembly places, rest, and feeding centres, including schools, church rooms and public buildings served by 247 volunteers and members of the Women's Voluntary Service (now the Royal Voluntary Service).

The headquarters and control centre was Hendford Manor; it was staffed by one sub-controller, two deputies, ten assistants and sixty-eight telephonists and other jobs.

Yeovil's civil defence services (excluding fire and police) included a small number of full-time paid staff but the majority were volunteers, and at the beginning of 1943 numbered just over 8,000 men and women; all stood down at the end of the war in 1945.

Anti-Aircraft Defence

The Balloon Barrage

The Royal Air Force Balloon Barrages were a form of static defence designed to force enemy aircraft to fly higher and therefore bomb less accurately or deter dive-bombing attacks. The LZ (low zone) balloon, the main component of the barrages, was approximately 62 feet long and 25 feet in diameter filled with hydrogen gas. With three air-filled stabilising fins, the balloon was designed to fly at an altitude of 5,000 feet attached by a steel cable to a mobile winch.

The balloon barrages were controlled by Balloon Command, divided into groups and Balloon Barrage squadrons. Initially, the balloon barrage was formed to defend London but was soon extended to major provincial cities, and on 31 May 1940, the Air Ministry instructed the barrage to cover factories engaged in the vital task of aircraft production, including the Westland Works at Yeovil.

On 24 July 1940, No. 957 (Balloon) Squadron arrived in Yeovil with twenty-four balloons; squadron headquarters was established in 'Braggchurch', Hendford Hill. During the next four years, the barrage balloon sites set up in and around the town included Aldon, Barwick Park, Bunford, Coronation Avenue, East Coker Road/Sandhurst Road, Grass Royal, Higher Kingston Recreation Ground, Larkhill Lane, Lufton Camp, Marlclose, Preston Grove, West Hendford, Westland Works, and Yew Tree Close.

The barrage was raised when enemy aircraft were reported to be approaching Yeovil, and even without hostile activity, the flying of the barrage was not without incident. Balloons were vulnerable to lighting strike and high winds; there was also the danger of machine gun attack by enemy aircraft. In March and April 1941 alone, five balloons were destroyed by lightning and one broke adrift in a high wind to come down in East Chinnock.

On 7 October 1940, following the first heavy air raid on Yeovil, there was an unexploded bomb by the Larkhill Lane site. The crew of the balloon at Yew Tree Close had a lucky escape on the night of 8 May 1941, when a German bomber struck the cable and dropped its bombs on the site. Fortunately, there were no casualties, but the crew's accommodation hut was smashed. There were reports of the balloon barrage being machine gunned on 9 August 1942. Repairs to the balloons were carried out in St Michael's Hall as this was the only building in the town with sufficient internal length and height to enable the balloon to be inflated to check the repair.

In June 1944, the Germans unleashed their V-1 flying bombs on London and the Home Counties, and on 21 June, No. 957 Squadron was sent to the south coast to join the 'Anti-Diver' measures set up to combat this menace.

Anti-Aircraft Guns (AA) and Searchlights

During 1940, anti-aircraft (AA) guns were brought to defend the Westland Works and located around the area. Four heavy 3.7-inch AA guns were installed on the Showground by the Dorchester Road, and Bofors Light AA guns were placed on various sites, including one at the top of Hendford Hill near the Quicksilver Mail public house, and another next to the bridge over the now disused railway line by Bunford Lane on the south side of the airfield. Positions were also set up for machine guns. The guns were manned by Regular soldiers and members of the local home guard. Owing to the temporary nature of the gun positions no evidence remains.

Searchlights also formed part of anti-aircraft defences, and with their strong beams of light, they sought out enemy aircraft at night for the anti-aircraft guns to attempt to shoot down. The searchlight batteries were mobile and placed near potential targets such as the Westland Works. No evidence remains of the searchlight batteries set up around Yeovil, but a Somerset Civil Defence report on 7 May 1941 tells of an enemy plane over Yeovil firing down a searchlight beam and then seen to crash in flames to the east.

The Royal Observer Corps

An important element in the nation's anti-aircraft defences was the Royal Observer Corps (the title 'Royal' was granted in 1941), which provided a nationwide, round-the-clock system of spotting and identifying enemy aircraft crossing the country and was essential for the efficient operation of the air raid warning system. The corps (which was primarily staffed by volunteers) identified, tracked, and reported the passage of all aircraft, friend or foe, from observer posts on high hills or other prominent positions, in clusters of two to four posts, linked to group centres that passed the information to fighter group and sector operations rooms and up to Fighter Command. No. 22 Group centre was located at the top of the Southwoods cul-de-sac, off Hendford Hill.

The Royal Observer Corps was 'stood down' on 12 May 1945, four days after VE-Day, but with the threat from the Soviet Union and nuclear war, the corps was reactivated in 1947. From 1957 to 1991, the corps was given the important role of measuring and reporting on the onset, location, and aftereffects of a possible nuclear attack. However, with the collapse of the Soviet Union and the advance of technology to detect nuclear explosions and fallout, the corps was 'stood down' in 1991. The Southwoods group HQ was completely rebuilt in 1963 and closed some years ago. The reconstructed building is now a private residence.

Camouflage

During the Second World War, many forms of camouflage were used extensively to break up the forms of buildings or otherwise disguise them from the prying eyes of enemy aircraft. One method was to paint factory and commercial buildings to resemble domestic property. Several large workshop buildings and hangars at Westland Aircraft were camouflaged to resemble houses and the aerodrome marked out to represent agricultural fields. The large bulk of the former Gaumont Cinema in South Street was camouflaged to represent two detached houses, and the faint outlines can still be seen on the south wall from the Stars Lane car park.

Not every camouflage plan, however, met with public approval. In the dangerous summer of 1940, it was believed in some quarters that white houses should be darkened as they were thought to be conspicuous targets for night bombers, and some cottages had their lime-washed covered with black tar, but to one unnamed correspondent, writing in the press in August 1940:

It seemed difficult to believe that scattered white houses dimly visible and very small indeed to an observer several hundred feet up would be of any use at all to an enemy bomber searching for a large factory or other military objective and it seems unlikely that they would waste bombs on such ridiculous targets. Moonlight reflected on the crowded slate roofs of towns, especially if wet, on rivers, canals and railway lines and concrete roads are but a few of the objects which would be more effective as guides to the enemy.

As lime-washed walls were such a feature of many English landscapes, the Council for the Preservation of Rural England requested a ruling from the camouflage division of the Ministry of Home Security, who confirmed that such camouflaging was unnecessary, and thousands of white houses and cottages, including some on the highest points of Yeovil, were spared the indignity of being sprayed with tar.

The Dunkirk Spirit

On 31 May 1940, the evacuation of the BEF was taking place from the beaches and port of Dunkirk, and the operation that began on 27 May would continue until 3 June, by which time some 200,000 British and 140,000 French troops would be brought back to our shores. Mr Winston Churchill, the prime minister, would tell the nation that now the Battle of France was over, the Battle of Britain was about to begin. However, throughout these desperate times, the local columns of the *Western Gazette* would continue to report the everyday events in Yeovil and how life carried on with some semblance of normality.

Reg Allen's school of dancing announced that as from 1 June, classes would be held every Saturday at 8.15 p.m. in the guide hut at Everton Road instead of St Andrew's Hall. The Yeovil Girl Guides held a whist drive in the guide hut and the proceeds went towards the national fund for purchasing two air ambulances and a motor lifeboat.

The Huish Baptist and Preston Road Methodist Sunday schools celebrated their anniversaries, and the Salvation Army Temple held its anniversary service on 9 June. The Vicarage Street Methodist Choir—assisted by Mr Gerald Ricketts (tenor) and Mr Roy Slade (violin)—gave a musical hour with a silver collection. Popular concerts by the Yorke Variety Orchestra were held in the grounds of Hendford Manor and at Sidney Gardens. Doris Waller was the 'Popular Soprano' vocalist, and proceeds from both concerts were sent the lord mayor of London's Red Cross Appeal.

The Artisans' Golf club held its annual meeting in the clubhouse, with Mr W. J. C. Pittard, captain of the Yeovil Golf club, presiding. A vote of thanks was given to the Yeovil golf club for their proposal to reduce the subscription for members joining the armed forces, and it was agreed to make them honorary members of the artisans' club for the duration of the war.

St John's gym held a dance in St Andrew's Hall, with Norman Harvey as MC. Over 150 danced to Eddie Dyer's Band and £5 was raised for gym funds. A leather attaché case was presented to John Willey, the 'youthful social secretary' for organising dances, in aid of various charities.

A talk on the development of destroyers and the work and life on board them, was given by a naval officer, unnamed for security reasons, to the weekly meeting of Yeovil Rotary club on 4 June. Captain A. L. Pavey, in thanking the speaker, said that recent events performed by the Royal Navy had made the country prouder of the service than at any time since 1918.

Fire broke out in the Three Choughs hotel but was quickly put out by the fire brigade before much damage could be done. The appropriately named chef, Mr L. Fryer, had been awakened by the smell of smoke, and with other members of the hotel staff, he kept the fire under control until the brigade arrived. The *Western Gazette* reported that it had not been necessary to wake the guests, and many were unaware of what had happened. However, despite these signs of normality, the grave situation facing the nation sat side by side in the columns of the *Gazette*.

For some years following the end of the First World War, a captured German field gun had stood as a trophy of war in Bide's Garden (now part of the Reckleford dual carriageway in front of the hospital), and following a proposition by Councillor H. E. Higdon, the borough council decided to hand it back to the government 'for war purposes'.

Several contingents of the BEF evacuated from Dunkirk were camped in and around the town, and many older Yeovilians can remember seeing soldiers resting in the streets still with the grime of battle on their uniforms. All the Yeovil churches and chapels responded to a national day of prayer; the vicar of Yeovil, Preb. A. Chisholm, speaking in St. John's, welcomed members of the BEF present in the congregation and assured them that the town was grateful for their heroic services and trusted that their stay would provide the rest they richly deserved. The quick whip-round of the weekend shifts at Westland Aircraft collected over £100 for members of the BEF, and a voucher was given to every returned soldier in the town, including the wounded men in the district hospital.

A local casualty of war was cyclist Horace Culverhouse (of 19 Crofton Avenue), who was taken to hospital suffering from injuries to his face and legs when he collided in the dark with a barbed-wire roadblock on the Dorchester Road; he was allowed home after treatment.

Although there were 240 air raid wardens in Yeovil, volunteers were still urgently required for the warden service, first-aid parties, gas contamination squads, and control room telephonists for night duty; an appeal went out for people to come forward to fill the posts. The response was immediate and overwhelming. At the end of May, fifty-seven local men had been registered as conscientious objectors out of the 2,250 men registered service under the Military Training Act.

A sapper of the Royal Engineers was brought before the town magistrates charged with stealing a car from Goldcroft and driving when uninsured and without a licence. The arresting officer stated that when the accused had been detained near Salisbury, he said that he had stolen the car to get to London to see his relatives as he had just been evacuated with the BEF after a rough time over there and wanted a couple of days of leave. The sapper told the bench that he had been in France for six months and had got back to England on 31 May. He had only been lounging about in the camp, otherwise he would not have taken the car. Alderman W. J. C. Pittard told the sapper that 'We thank all the BEF for what they have done and for that reason we could not possibly see our way to punish you.' The charges were dismissed.

Rumour and gossip are always present at a time of war, and 'Silentium' wrote to the *Western Gazette*:

Could not the Mayor, or some other responsible person, follow the example of the Mayor of Southampton and institute an 'anti-gossip' week in Yeovil. It is badly needed. The amount of gossip regarding Westlands, where troops are &c., would keep and 'Fifth Columnist' busy recording it. Also, the amount of 'scare gossip' which is also very prevalent must be doing a lot of harm.

There were spy scares galore, and Mrs Knight of 52 West Hendford went so far as to insert the following notice in the *Gazette* on 31 May denying that 'Miss Fordham who has recently lived with her, has masqueraded as a man, or has acted as a spy, while staying at her house. The lady has been proved to be a highly-respected British retired business woman of Grays, Essex.'

However, the war could be forgotten for a few hours at the cinema in the first week of June 1940. Boris Karloff was appearing in *Mr. Wong at Headquarters* and Randolph Scott in *20,00 Men A Year* at the Gaumont; Basil Rathbone was *Sherlock Holmes* at the Odeon; and *The All Star All-Women Sensation—The Women* was showing three times a day at the Central cinema in Church Street.

The Home Guard

The German Army's overwhelming onslaught in the West during April and early May 1940 brought with it the real fear of an invasion of these shores. As the situation worsened, there was great concern at the state of the country's defences and the corresponding need for a local defence force.

On 14 May, the secretary of state for war, Mr Anthony Eden, appealed on the radio for 'Large numbers of men in Great Britain, who are British subjects, between the ages of 17 and 65 to come forward now and offer their services in order to make assurance doubly sure. The name of the new Force will be "The Local Defence Volunteers".' (LDV). Within days, tens of thousands of volunteers, many veterans of the First World War, had come forward, and with the evacuation of the BEF from Dunkirk and the fall of France, Great Britain stood alone.

During the summer of 1940, the LDV was formed into battalions, companies, and platoons attached to their local areas; two months later, on 22 July, the name was changed to the home guard. Arming and clothing the home guard presented a major problem during those early months, but by the end of 1940, it had become a credible fighting force. However, the home guard was not to be tested as the feared invasion never came.

In Somerset, the battalions were established across the county and Yeovil was part of the 3rd Somerset (Yeovil) Battalion, Home Guard, commanded by Lt-Colonel G. H. G. Ing, CMG, DSO, DL, with its headquarters at 11 Summerlands, Preston Road, Yeovil. The Yeovil borough company was commanded by the town clerk, Major H. C. C. Batten, DSO, with the company headquarters in the King George Street Municipal Offices. Major Batten would become the second in command of the 3rd Somerset Battalion and Major C. E. Almer, MC, succeeded to the command of the borough company.

The battalion also included the Westland (Works) Company and companies at Queen Camel, Ilchester, Stoke-sub-Hamdon (Hamdon), Crewkerne, and Heron (RNAS); there was also an auxiliary unit, a resistance group who would cause damage and disruption to the enemy.

From January 1941, in the event of invasion, Yeovil would form an 'anti-tank island' defended by the Borough company supported by the 208th LAA Training Regiment, Royal Artillery from Houndstone Camp. The anti-tank island comprised a pillbox strong-point on Summerhouse Hill covering approaches from the south in the direction of Barwick along with an outer and inner circle of roadblocks designed to hold up and delay the passage of enemy tanks and other vehicles approaching from the south or west. The outer roadblocks would be placed at the top of Hendford Hill supported by a pillbox strong-point in the front garden of no. 166 and at Newton Road railway bridge. The inner roadblocks, at which anti-tank obstacles of triangular iron rails and concrete tubes would be placed, were at Huish near the junction with West Street; West Street; Westland Road near the junction with Beer Street; Beer Street near the junction with West Hendford; West Hendford near the junction with Beer Street; Hendford near the junction with Brunswick Street; Brunswick Street near the junction with Penn Hill; Addlewell Lane, northern and southern ends; Stars Lane near the junction with Summerhouse Terrace; Station Road near the junction with Middle Street; Newton Road near the junction with Sherborne Road; and the reserve and quartermaster's stores in the Southville drill hall.

Thankfully the invasion never came, and the Yeovil anti-tank island was never put to the test. However, the Summerhouse Hill pillbox still stands looking south towards Barwick and the Dorset Hills—the feared invasion route.

The home guard became an important part of the nation's armed forces, releasing the regular army to take the war to the enemy. They patrolled and guarded important places such as airfields, factories, and communication centres; the home guard also manned anti-aircraft guns and coastal defence artillery batteries, being credited with shooting down a number of enemy aircraft.

However, following the success of the D-Day on 6 June 1944 and the Allied advance through France to Germany, the home guard formally stood down on 3 December 1944. Nationally, 1,206 men died on duty and all who served three or more years were awarded the Defence Medal. Jeffrey Wilson's book *The Somerset Home Guard—A Pictorial Roll Call* (published by Millstream Books in 2004) is an excellent account of the Somerset Home Guard.

Air Raid Shelters

With the fall of France in June 1940, the whole of the south and west of England was well within the range of German bombers, and attacks began on Somerset with bombs on Flax Bourton, near Bristol, on 18 June. Yeovil had already put in hand plans to provide air raid shelters, and on 4 July 1940, the borough council announced in the *Western Gazette* that shelters were available for 1,195 people in specially adapted cellars in business and private premises. The council stated, however, that the shelters were for people who might be caught in the streets during an air raid, and not for the protection of nearby residents.

The shelters were provided in the following premises: 19 High Street; Western Counties Stores, Church Street entrance; Redwoods, The Borough; Harbour and Hobbs, Vicarage Street; Confectionery Dept., Co-operative Society, Middle Street; Bakery Dept., Co-operative Society, Vicarage Street; Dunn & Co. Middle Street (rear entrance Vicarage Street); Brutton's Cellars, Clarence Street; British Legion, Princes Street; Dr Unwin, Kingston House, Kingston; Mr T. Moore's Stables, Higher Kingston; Holman & Ney's, Hendford; Dupont, 63 Hendford; and Brooks, Dentist, Hendford. Under construction were Radio House, Princes Street at the entrance to Quik Auto Motor Body Works, Park Road; 13 Kingston adjoining Duke of York Inn; and Mr Buchanan's House, North Lane.

In giving these details in its July edition, the *Yeovil Review* advised housewives and others likely to be in the town during the day to cut out the article and carry it with them so that they would be acquainted with the exact location of the shelter should the occasion arise.

At the meeting of the borough council on 9 September, the mayor stated his concern:

> The behaviour of certain irresponsible people in the air raid shelters which was absolutely disgusting and decent people refused to use the shelters. It was only a small percentage of people who made themselves a complete nuisance to others and he hoped they would remain outside and expose themselves to whatever dangers existed.

On 9 November 1940, it was reported that shelters had been provided for 2,900 people and accommodation for another 500 was under construction. By 10 February 1941, the borough council announced that the total number of domestic, communal and other forms of shelter could now accommodate 3,075, with work in hand for another 1,704. However, the misuse of public shelters continued, and it was reported that three had to be thoroughly scrubbed out and cleansed before they could be used.

A report to the borough council's invasion committee on 30 September 1942 on the provision of air raid shelters in Yeovil stated that the total number of persons who could be accommodated had reached 16,233 in mainly in domestic surface shelters and Anderson and Morrison shelters.

The surface domestic shelter was generally constructed of brick or concrete block and was designed to withstand all but the direct hit from a bomb. The shelters were usually erected in the back gardens of houses and shared by several householders and their families.

Anderson shelters were issued free early in the war to householders and comprised a number of curved sheets of corrugated iron assembled to form an arch with wooden ends, one being used as the entrance. The shelter was sunk into the ground, usually in the back garden, and covered with a protective layer of earth.

The Morrison shelter was for use indoors and named after Mr Herbert Morrison, the home secretary in 1941 when the shelters were issued free to householders. The shelter, which was assembled by the householder, comprised four welded mesh sides and base with a strong solid metal top. As with most surface air raid shelters, the Morrison could not protect its occupants from a direct bomb hit but provided substantial protection from falling masonry in the event of a near miss.

On 11 September 1944, following the advance of the Allied armies across France and into Belgium, the threat of air attack on Yeovil had become virtually non-existent and the borough council decided to close all public air raid shelters.

In 1947, the communal domestic air raid shelters were sold to the householder on whose land each stood for the sum of £1 1s, and many of the brick or concrete structures can still be found serving a variety of domestic purposes.

October: The First Air Raids

During the Second World War, Somerset was not spared the attentions of the German Luftwaffe. Air attacks began in June 1940 and continued with varying degrees of severity until May 1944. The cities of Bristol and Bath were heavily bombed and suffered grievously. Attacks by bomb and gunfire on Somerset ranged from Weston-super-Mare to Castle Cary, Bridgwater to Montacute, and cost the lives of 668 of its people with a further 1,608 injured and some 35,000 buildings destroyed or damaged.

In Yeovil, air raid warning sirens were sounded on 365 occasions from Friday, 5 July 1940 to Friday, 16 June 1944. People took to the air raid shelters listening for the sound of approaching enemy aircraft and wondering whether bombs would fall on the town. On 355 occasions, the enemy passed over heading for Bristol, the cities and ports of South Wales, the north-west of England, or some other target. Quite often, the raiders did not come; it might be a false alarm or the enemy changed direction. The length of time between the warning and the 'all clear' being sounded could last for hours or a few minutes. During the night of 16–17 January 1940, the warning lasted for nearly eleven hours, whereas it was only five minutes on the following 22 March.

On Monday, 30 September 1940, a force of German bombers set out to attack the Westland Aircraft Works at Yeovil, but heavy clouds covered the target, and bombing blind, the aircraft released their bombs over Sherborne causing considerable damage, killing eighteen and injuring thirty townspeople. With the aircraft works being the obvious target, it was only a matter of time before the Luftwaffe returned and the town would suffer ten air raids during the coming two years.

Monday, 7 October 1940 was the 401st day of the war, and at 3.45 p.m., the air raid sirens wailed their warning over Yeovil. Townspeople hurried to take shelter, and some ten minutes later, over twenty German Ju 88 bombers approached the town from the east—Yeovil was now in the front line as high explosive and oil firebombs rained destruction across the town centre and nearby residential areas.

A direct hit demolished the air raid shelter in the Vicarage Street Methodist church, killing four housewives and injuring several of the thirty or so people who had taken refuge in the building. A man, two women, and an eighteen-month-old toddler were trapped for a while in a cavity formed by fallen blocks of masonry but were released relatively unharmed.

In Middle Street, a bomb exploded between Montague Burton's shop and Woolworths store, killing eight people, including two young men who had been playing billiards in the saloon above Burton's. Miraculously, most of the 200 people sheltering in Woolworths escaped injury.

The fall of bombs across the town centre damaged shops and business premises but thankfully with no further fatalities. The *Western Gazette* reported that a young chemist's assistant experienced his second bombing within a week having transferred to Yeovil from a shop in another town damaged in a raid. Ricketts' glove factory in Addlewell Lane was badly damaged but once again, mercifully without serious casualties.

Bombs, including an oil bomb, fell on the Higher Kingston Estate and a house in Roping Road was demolished. However, the bombs that fell on the western parts of Yeovil caused further deaths and injuries. Baker's roundsman, Cyril Rendell from West Coker, was killed in Summerleaze Park where he was delivering bread; a direct hit on an air raid shelter in Grove Avenue killed the two occupants; and a housewife died when her house in St Andrew's Road was blown apart. An oil bomb bounced down Grove Avenue, and there was a large crater left in a vacant piece of land opposite the entrance to West Park; craters also pitted the playing fields around Summerleaze Park school, now Oaklands primary school. Several houses in St Andrew's Road still bear shrapnel marks from the bombs that fell nearby. There was an unexploded bomb at the junction of Preston and St Andrew's Roads, another in Park Street, and a third in the field near the balloon barrage site at Larkhill; an oil bomb that fell in Everton Road failed to explode.

The *Western Gazette* reported that two insurance agents had a narrow escape when an oil bomb fell three feet away from the front door of one of a row of houses. It blew in the door behind which they were sheltering at the invitation of an evacuee from London, who was the only other person in the house. They were all three thrown to the floor, the door falling on top of them. Splinters from a bomb went straight through the rear of the car the men had left outside, and another large pieced the roof and landed on the driver's seat. Oily mud thickly splattered the car. Luckily, the bomb did not ignite, although the force of the explosion was sufficient to break the concrete doorstep and tear laths from the wooden shed at the rear of the house.

The bombers were gone in minutes and when the 'all clear' sounded an hour later, sixteen people were dead and twenty-nine injured, of whom nine were serious; not one bomb had hit the Westland Aircraft Works.

The sixteen people who lost their lives were: Mrs F. Lumber, Mrs W. Bright, Mrs V. Pickard and Mrs M. Bugler (air raid shelter at Vicarage Street Methodist Church); Mr R. Batstone, Mrs F. Batstone, Mr A. Palmer; Mr F. Rose, Mr N. Gay, Mr W. Tucker, Mrs E. Smith, and Mrs L. Johnson (Montague Burton's shop); Mr C. Rendell (Summerleaze Park); Mrs A. Hayward (25 St Andrew's Road); and Mr L. Forsey and Mrs M. Morris (Air raid shelter at 45 Grove Avenue).

The Luftwaffe came again the next evening, and between ten past seven, when the sirens wailed the alert, until the 'all clear,' forty-five minutes later, some forty-four high explosive bombs were scattered over the western part of Yeovil. This time, Preston Grove and Westbourne Grove bore the brunt of the attack and once again the Westland Works remained unscathed. The raid left eleven dead, all killed when an air raid shelter at the corner of Westbourne Grove and Preston Grove was totally destroyed by a direct hit. Eight of those who died, including two children, were soon identified, but early the following morning, an unidentifiable adult body was found in the St Andrew's Road cul-de-sac, followed shortly after by that of a badly mutilated child in a garden in Preston Grove; five days later, a mutilated female corpse was found on allotments by the Westland airfield. Despite extensive enquiries, the three bodies were never identified, and they were buried in Yeovil Cemetery where a headstone marks their last resting place.

The eleven people who lost their lives were: Mrs M. Heywood, Mrs M. Harrison, Mr W. Fitkin, Mrs O. Fitkin, Maxwell Fitkin (three years), Laurence Sweet (nine years), Miss J. Dodge, Miss J. Young, and the three unidentified bodies.

The third attack on Yeovil came on Saturday evening 12 October, when a lone bomber dropped five high explosive bombs on the town centre. Part of Church House, occupied by the solicitors Messrs Batten & Co., was demolished and the south windows in St. John's Church were damaged. The *Western Gazette* reported that the glass canopy over the entrance to 'a picture theatre was shattered and some tiles dislodged but that was the extent of the damage. No-one in the cinema was hurt and the show went on.' This was the Central cinema on Church Street, but wartime censorship forbade the naming of towns, streets etc in newspaper reports of air raids. The film showing at the time was *Jack's the Boy* starring Jack Hulbert and Cicely Courtneidge. The other bombs fell in Park Street and at the back of a house in Pen Hill, demolishing part of the building and damaging the adjoining South Street infants school; there were five reported injuries in the town.

Houndstone camp was bombed on 12 October when five soldiers were killed and thirty-two other personnel were injured, and again on the fourteenth, when thirteen died, including Lt-Col. G.F.R. Wingate OBE, a relative of Major General Orde Wingate, leader of the famous 'Chindits' of the Burma campaign. The Lt-Col. and a number of soldiers killed in this raid lie buried in the Commonwealth War Graves Commission's plot in Yeovil Cemetery.

The fourth raid on the town came on 16 October when bombs fell in Mudford Road, destroying five houses and injuring three occupants of no. 122. Although this would be the last attack on Yeovil in 1940, the air raid warnings would be given on another twenty-eight occasions before the end of the year as the Luftwaffe passed overhead to bomb Bristol and South Wales.

In the four raids on Yeovil in 1940, twenty-seven premises were totally destroyed and over 800 damaged, but the target—the Westland factory— was unscathed. However, more raids would follow in 1941 and 1942.

Around the Town in 1940

War on Hooligans

In January 1940, the *Yeovil Review* declared 'War on Hooliganism':

> It would be a pity if the war is going to mean an outbreak in Yeovil of that type of senseless and wanton hooliganism on a par with German 'frightfulness' from which this town has hitherto been almost completely free.
>
> During the past week or so there have been glaring examples of malicious damage to cars, shop windows as well as to trees and shrubs in public parks.
>
> Three motorists found their cars almost wrecked. Tyres were slashed, leads torn out, windscreens and windows smashed, and in addition to their damage the tanks were filled with gravel and mud.
>
> Such senseless acts can only be described as the work of maniacs, while the wilful smashing of shop windows with beer bottles is hooliganism at its worst.
>
> The trouble now appears to have spread to public parks, on Christmas day seats in Preston Park were overturned and some thrown in the pond.
>
> So determined are the Council to stamp out this wrecking campaign that it has been decided to offer a reward for information that will lead to the apprehension of the culprits.
>
> When they appear before the local magistrates, it is hoped that the punishment meted out will be of such a nature as to indicate in the clearest possible manner that Yeovil is not going to stand behaviour of a kind only to be found in the lowest part of Limehouse.

Sadly, much of the vandalism occurring in the town was blamed on the evacuees, quite wrongly in most cases.

Sunday Cinemas

The *Yeovil Review* commented:

Those people who thought that Sunday Cinemas were not needed in Yeovil must have received a shock when they saw the length of the queues outside the two picture houses [the Odeon and Gaumont]. Nor is it simply because pictures on a Sunday are a novelty. Ever since Sunday opening has been in operation there have been full houses in spite of the fact that the lighter evenings are here.

One thing Sunday Cinemas have done, and that is put an end to the Sunday night parade in Middle Street and other main thoroughfares, when young people with nowhere to go and nothing to do spend the time aimlessly wandering the streets. The soldiers, for whose benefit Sunday cinemas have been provided, have not been slow to show their appreciation as is evidenced by the large proportion of khaki in the audiences.

When the application for Sunday films was made, local cinema managers, suggested 6 o'clock opening, but this was turned down in favour of 7.30 opening as it was feared that church attendances would suffer.

It would appear, in view of the large assembly of people outside the cinemas from 6 p.m. onwards that the suggestion of the managers was, after all, quite a sensible one. Perhaps in view of the experience gained a revision of the opening time may be possible.

This is what our Sunday cinema-goers enjoyed during May 1940: on 12 May, Gaumont showed *Four's a Crowd* and *Adventures of Jane Ard* while Odeon showed *Carefree* and *Pecks Bad Boy at the Circus*. On 19 May, Gaumont showed *Heart of the North* and *Gentleman's Gentleman* while Odeon showed *Gangs of New York* and *Romance on the Run*. On 26 May, Gaumont showed *Gold is where you find it* and *Back to Nature* while Odeon showed *Story of Irene and Vernon Castle* and *Arizona Legion*.

A Warning to Allotment Holders

The *Yeovil Review* reported:

The biggest nightmare the 'Dig for Victory' enthusiasts could have been surely to discover, after hours of hard work when their back is almost ready to break and they are so dry that beer tax or no, they feel they must quench their thirst in an extra-large tankard of mild and bitter, that they have been digging not their own allotment but someone else's. This what really happened to a certain allotment enthusiast. Anxious to do his bit for his country in the 'Dig for Victory' campaign he decided after his day's work was done to get busy by night on the land. He obtained a plot on one of the Corporation allotments and took up his gardening in deadly earnest, putting several hours of hard digging, preparing the ground for cropping. Delighted with the result of his first night's efforts he received the surprise of his life.

A neighbouring allotment holder came up and warmly thanked him for the splendid job he had made of it. 'You have made my allotment look the neatest up here,' he said. Realising that he had been digging somebody else's allotment the enthusiast was on the point of collapse and wonder.

The comedy of the whole thing was that the allotment he had been digging was the worst of the lot.

Long Life in Yeovil

The *Yeovil Review* commented:

Rationing and other war-time difficulties have meant that many peace time social functions and other annual events have had to be dropped for the duration, but the Baptist Fellowship saw to it that the Old Folks had their annual party 'War or no war' in the South Street Schools where well over two hundred Old Yeovilians of both sexes were enjoying themselves quite as much as any youngsters would.

Attracted by the sounds of merriment one or two 'Kilties' looked in to see what it was all about and this led to one old lady to remark to her friends 'Who be they there boys wi' petticoats on.'

The oldest guest of the party was Mr. W. Russell, who is 89, and he and Mrs. Hill, who is 88, were each presented with a cake by Mrs. Frank Clothier. A bouquet was sent to Mrs. Patten who has attained her 93rd birthday and was unable to be at the party owing to ill-health.

It speaks of the healthiness of Yeovil that the average age of the guests was 71. In fact we might have a new slogan: 'If you want to live long come to Yeovil.'

Fashion

Looking at one of the twenty-first-century fashions of torn designer jeans, those who favour them might feel at home in May 1940, although the designer tears would not be allowed to last long in the make do and mend spirit of the time as shown in this *Yeovil Review* article:

> Dame Fashion may decree that dresses should be worn shorter, but women may also find it necessary to wear them longer.
>
> Drapery stores have laid in big stocks so that the Board of Trade's new Order restricting wholesalers' sales of cotton, rayon and linen goods to 75 per cent. of pre-war quantities is not expected to result in any shortages this summer. But if any future shortage is to be avoided, clothes will have to last a little longer.
>
> In other words the motto must be 'mend instead of spend.' The slogan 'Darn for Victory,' may indeed become as well-known as 'Dig for Victory.' Don't mind having a homely patch here and there. When victory comes and you blossom out in a gorgeous new outfit you will be proud of your self-sacrifice.
>
> Almost everything a woman wears is affected by the restrictions—blouses, dresses and lingerie, but mere man is not to go scot-free either. He will find that his shirts also come under the Order, though to the same degree.
>
> But there is the consolation of knowing that he will not have to wear 'Ersatz' frocks and shirts like the Germans, when the effect of a shower of rain on paper-made clothing might well mean a minor tragedy, especially on Sunday morning church parade.

The columnist could not have foreseen five more years of total war, and his lady readers would have to wait a little longer to blossom out in gorgeous new outfits.

5

1941

Some Important Events

27 March	German Afrika Corps start offensive in North Africa.
6 April	Germany invades Yugoslavia and Greece.
31 May	British army surrenders on Crete.
1 June	Clothes rationing begins.
22 June	Operation Barbarossa: German invasion of Soviet Union.
7 December	Japanese attack Pearl Harbor and declare war on the United States of America.
8 December	USA and her Allies (except Soviet Union) declare war on Japan; Japanese invade Malaya.
25 December	Hong Kong surrenders to the Japanese Army.

The National Fire Service

The Yeovil volunteer fire brigade was founded in 1862 and remained a part-time volunteer brigade until the outbreak of war in September 1939, when the chief fire officer, Mr C. O. Mitchell, and eight of the regular volunteers were employed and paid full-time.

In 1938, following the fears of widespread aerial attack, the Government established the volunteer part-time Auxiliary Fire Service (AFS) in every city and town to support the regular brigades. By September 1939, there were seventy AFS volunteers in Yeovil, nine of whom were made full-time paid firefighters and joined their colleagues in the town brigade.

The heavy air raids during 1940 and early 1941 saw local brigades assisting neighbouring city or town units but it was soon found that the many different brigades and incompatible equipment greatly reduced their effectiveness. In August 1941, the National Fire Service (NFS) was created by the amalgamation of the AFS with the 1,600 or so local authority brigades. The resulting standardisation of training, equipment and control provided the ability for re-enforcements to be sent wherever they were needed. The Yeovil contingent, supported by the town's voluntary aid ambulances and first aiders, would render assistance at Bristol, Exeter, and Plymouth before and after the establishment of the NFS.

The formation of the NFS saw Yeovil become No. 2 sub-division of Area 8 of Region 7 with its headquarters in the pre-war South Street fire station and the borough of Yeovil War Book 1943 states that an alternative control room had been established at Mudford Road opposite the entrance to Combe Street Lane, an 'Action Station' in Sparrows' motor garage and showrooms on Sherborne Road, and seven sub-stations at other locations in the town. There were ten fire engines and an escape unit together with a number of heavy vehicles including a hosepipe carrier, a hosepipe layer, a foam tender, and an articulated lorry loaded with 1 mile of six-inch steel pipe to carry water pumped from the River Yeo. Although the majority of the fire engines and the heavy equipment was stationed at South Street, there were several heavy units at Sherborne Road, and a further seven light trailer pumps positioned in the sub-stations. There were ninety-two full-time NFS personnel, including nineteen firewomen and 159 part-timers with twenty-eight firewomen and seventeen messengers. When 'Action Stations' was called, neighbouring units would come to support the town.

In 1948, the NFS stood down and the fire service was placed under the control of county and county borough councils. Patrol officer Charles Gillard of the AFS was the only Yeovil fireman to lose his life during the war when he was killed by the explosion of a delayed action bomb as he fought the resulting fire in the Corn Exchange during the 1941 Good Friday air raid. On the piece of the remaining Corn Exchange wall, there is a plaque, which reads: 'In memory of CHARLES GILLARD Yeovil Fireman killed here performing his duty during bombing raid 12th April 1941.'

A major problem in fighting fires was the disruption of water supplies due to the destruction of water mains, and in Yeovil, as in other cities and towns, a large number of alternative sources were provided. The town's resources varied from tanks in factory premises, static water tanks placed on land at strategic points, to the River Yeo, local streams, and ponds. Many local people may well remember some of the static water tanks that were retained in the 1950s arising from the fears of nuclear attack during the Cold War.

The Five Air Raids of 1941

On Wednesday 26 March 1941, Yeovil suffered its fifth air raid in the Second World War. Once again, the Westland Aircraft Works was the target.

At 11 o'clock on that Wednesday morning, the air raid warning wailed across Yeovil, and one hour later, a lone Dornier bomber dived east to west over the town and dropped a stick of six high-explosive bombs. Four of the bombs fell on the nearby Westland housing estate and two fell in the works. When the all clear sounded at 1 o'clock, three men, five women and a five-year-old boy were dead and thirty-six civilians injured; four of the dead were Westland employees. Eleven houses were destroyed and one hundred and thirty-two damaged.

The official summary of the raid reported that one 250-kg bomb had penetrated the roof of the sub-assembly shop at an angle, struck the ground 180 feet from where it entered, ricocheted, and travelled for 240 feet, exploding opposite 'the office building where nearly all the windows (front and back) were broken by blast. Walls were heavily marked by splinters. In the erection shop, a large number of holes made by splinters, resulted in work being held up for a night.'

The second and smaller bomb of 50 kg 'Fell in the Flying Ground, skidded and exploded. Crater 4 feet × 6 feet. Water main damaged.'

Press reports of the time were heavily censored, and the places raided were never named or details given of factory or business premises. The *Western Gazette*'s report of the raid is therefore brief and does not say where it occurred:

Homes were damaged when a raider bombed and machine gunned a West Country town on Wednesday. Housewives were busily preparing the mid-day meal when an enemy 'plane dived out of the clouds and dropped its bombs on their homes. Many had miraculous escapes, but there were few casualties, some of them fatal.

A twenty-year-old girl who was to have been married at Easter, was among the killed. Another victim was a child. A woman whose home was extensively damaged, escaped injury by flinging herself under a table. One young mother dashed upstairs to save her baby, and threw herself across the cradle as the bombs were falling. Although her house was damaged, mother and child were unhurt. A machine gun attack accompanied the bombing. Bullets pierced the roof and also a window of a Roman Catholic Church, and they also shattered the windows of a club room, but no-one was injured. A man in a workshop had just moved away from his bench when bullets swept the spot where he had been working.

Eye-witnesses say that after carrying out its bombing and machine-gunning attack, the raider appeared to open out and make off at great speed.

The author's mother's parents lived in Westland Road and their house was damaged, but thankfully both were unhurt. However, when she went to make certain they were both all right following the 'all clear', she recalled seeing a 'snow storm' of feathers from destroyed pillowcases and eiderdowns blowing about in the wind.

One of the tragedies of that awful day was that of five-year-old Trevor Hoyle, who with his mother Lily, was killed when their house at 23 Westland Terrace received a direct hit; the remains of Lily Hoyle were recovered, but there was no sign of Trevor. Enquiries revealed that Trevor had been collected from Huish Infants school at about 11.45 a.m. by a mother who said she had come to collect her own child, and her friend Mrs Hoyle had asked her to collect Trevor as well. School rules only permitted a parent to collect a child from a primary school during the time an air raid warning was in force. However, Trevor was allowed to go with his mother's friend, but he was seen alone in Huish by a neighbour and by two air raid wardens in Westland Road. One of the wardens recalled seeing the little boy going down the cul-de-sac to his home shortly before the bombs fell. Questions were asked: why was Trevor seen on his own, and who or where was the mother who had collected him? Perhaps she was one of the casualties and could not answer the questions at the time; all we know is that five-year-old Trevor Hoyle's body was never found—he had just vanished.

The author has a brief memory of this raid. He was in the front room of his paternal grandparents' house on Beer Street and could recall a sudden shadow with lots of noise and then through the front room window, he saw an aircraft with two tail fins diving low over Westland Road and the bombs going down. He remembered being thrown to the floor by his father who was recovering from a second attack of rheumatic fever, a legacy of his service on the Western Front in the First World War. The author's father was staying at his parents' house because the under-stairs had been reinforced as an air raid shelter and the surface shelter at the bottom of the family's garden in nearby Orchard Street was too cold and damp.

Three men, five women, and the five-year-old boy were killed; four of the dead were Westland employees, and thirty-six were injured. In Westland Works, the casualties were Mrs H. Mulhall, Mrs M. Hann, Mr J. Palmer, and Mr L. Pritchard. In Westland Terrace, the casualties were Miss M. Guy, Mrs L. Hoyle, Trevor Hoyle (five years), Mrs J. Culvert, and Mr E. Neville.

The warning for the sixth raid was sounded at 9.40 p.m. in the evening of Good Friday, 11 April 1941, and by the time of the all clear, six hours later at 3 40. a.m., several delayed-action bombs had fallen and exploded in the town centre. The Corn Exchange, off High Street, and Boots the chemist, in the Borough, were destroyed; a large number of nearby premises, including shops, were damaged. The *Western Gazette* of 18 April recorded:

'Business as usual' notices in fashion stores typified the never-say-die spirit of local traders after high explosive bombs had been dropped by an enemy raider in a shopping district of a West Country town on the night of Good Friday.

One fire blazed like a beacon light but before it could be a guide to other raiders it had been extinguished by fire fighters, regular and auxiliary. When a high explosive made a direct hit on a three storey shop [this was Boots the Chemist and adjoining buildings on the Borough now Burger King] a mother and daughter, Mrs. Hawkins and Phyllis Hawkins, living in a flat on the top floor, were buried in wreckage, but after being extracted they were suffering only from shock. A bomb on another building caused a small number of casualties, some fatal. An A.F.S. man was also injured, but chatted cheerfully to ambulance men who took him to hospital.

A fire watcher at a large shop in the rear of which an H.E. bomb fell, perhaps owes his life to the failure of the store's electricity supply.

He is Bertram Francis, who was on duty with the night watchman when a bomb of the incendiary type fell by the cloakroom in the back of the shop and caused a fire. The two men immediately set to work with a stirrup pump, but their efforts were of no avail, and the Fire Brigade was called.

Meanwhile Francis went to the upstairs front of the building to try to rectify a fuse. While he was there, a bomb caused extensive damage to the rear of the shop where he had been fighting the fire previously.

Part of the staircase collapsed and Francis had to make his escape by way of the roof of adjoining buildings, ending with a climb part way down the face of a shop. He was helped the rest of the way by a party of helpers. With his companion he escaped injury. A street fire watcher who is a licensee, was caught by blast, and found himself on the ground unable to move in a road strewn with broken glass and other debris. 'I wondered what on earth had happened,' he said. 'I had to crawl to a hotel, windows of which had been blown out, but I found myself quite unhurt.' A curious experience befell a boy lying in bed in a flat over a nearby shop. The wardrobe suddenly fell across his bed with the door open. Part of the ceiling and walls collapsed, but the boy inside the wardrobe as it were—was not touched. Another tradesman had the double misfortune of seeing the wrecking of both his shop and his house at the rear. He and his wife had to be dug out but were unhurt. Windows of two churches in the area were found pitted with jagged holes.

The *Western Gazette*'s report that 'A bomb on another building caused a small number of casualties, some fatal', referred to the one that destroyed the Corn Exchange in which soldiers of the King's Own Scottish Borderers were billeted. Four unnamed soldiers were killed and five injured and patrol officer Charles Gillard of the AFS died when the delayed-action bomb exploded as he fought the fire in the Corn Exchange. The official summary of the raid suggested that incendiary bombs had been attached to the fins of the high-explosive bombs as the flames of the fire in the Corn Exchange were described as being of a 'yellow colour, as from a broken gas pipe. Water caused the fire to roar. This points to 0.9Kg I.B.'s attached to the fins as there were no gas mains in the vicinity'.

A memorial to patrol officer Gillard can be seen on the remains of the Corn Exchange wall adjoining the Borough Arcade between High Street and South Street.

The Good Friday raid left five dead and fourteen injured; seven buildings were totally destroyed and 182 were damaged.

The Luftwaffe would return for a seventh attack at midnight on 8 May when a lone bomber swept low over the town and became caught in the cable of a Royal Air Force barrage balloon at Yew Tree Close. The raider dropped its bombs but only succeeded in damaging the huts of the crew manning the balloon; there were no casualties.

Midnight on 16 May 1941, the 161st air raid warning of the war wailed over Yeovil, and about an hour later, a lone German bomber scattered seven high explosive bombs from Stone Lane to Mudford Road near the junction with St Michael's Avenue. The resulting explosions caused damage to the windows and doors of some sixty houses and the Fleur de Lys hotel; thankfully, there were no human casualties, but one innocent cow was killed with another injured. Yeovil had experienced its eighth air raid of the war, but a week later, the ninth, would be far more serious.

The air raid warning sounded at five minutes to midnight on Saturday 24 May and when the all clear sounded half-an-hour later, five people (including a nine-year-old boy) had been killed and seven injured. Eight houses at the top of Mudford Road had been totally destroyed or were so badly damaged they had to be demolished, and another 115 were damaged. The brief official reports of the raid state that at about two minutes past midnight a single enemy bomber dropped fourteen high-explosive bombs from a very low altitude after flying three times over the town with its navigation lights on.

Due to wartime censorship, the following report in the *Western Gazette* on 30 May was also brief and could not identify the town:

When high explosive bombs were dropped in the residential part of a West Country town on Saturday, a number of families were trapped in the wreckage of their homes. Heedless of their own safety neighbours assisted rescue squads, who worked desperately to extricate them. Casualties proved to be small, but included some killed. Among the victims were a husband and wife and the latter's sister. A nine years old boy was also fatally injured.

A soldier and his wife, had a remarkable escape. The wife had already been bombed out of a bungalow at which she had been staying in another town in order to be near her husband. She returned to her own home still suffering from shock. Her husband had been given compassionate leave to be with his wife who is ill. They were both in bed when the bombs fell. The bed slid to the ground, but they were both safe, though they now have no home and nothing but what they were wearing at the time.

A man owed his life to a wardrobe which fell on him and acted as a shield when his home was hit, and in another house nearby a woman was saved from injury by a door which was blown off its hinges on top of her as the ceiling collapsed. An invalid woman was found in bed unhurt amid the ruins of her home.

The raider was met by anti-aircraft fire. After dropping its bombs it quickly made off.

Salvage men, demolition crews, and other Civil Defence workers were all busy on Sunday, while husbands and wives, assisted by their children, spent the day in a great 'clean up'.

One of the casualties was Roy Bicknell, who was four years old at the time, and recalls that night:

With my mother and father I was living at 137 Mudford Road and we were amongst those injured in the bombing of 24 May and although I was only 4 years old at the time I have a vivid memory of that night. My father was home on leave as he was serving in the Royal Navy and had just come back from India. Although it is said that the alarm was sounded at 11.55pm I believe that the bombs had fallen before the alarm was sounded. A story I was told is that in the house opposite ours lived a woman who was bedridden and they had heard the plane going round above and she said to her husband to go to the shelter, but he said no, he would stay with her and if anything was to happen it would happen to them both. Their house was hit and they ended up in the road still on the bed with only minor cuts etc. and the people in the next houses either side were killed.

I had a bad cut to my right arm which was round my father's neck as he was carrying me to my Grandmother's shelter at 126 Mudford Road. We had got as far as the front gate of our home when the house opposite was hit, he also had injuries to his head and my mother had something skim over her and injure her back as we lay on the ground. We all made a complete recovery. Our home was damaged so much that after our stay in hospital we went to live in Goldcroft until our home was fit to live in after some months.'

The five fatal casualties were Mr and Mrs D. Haines, Miss K. Denmead, Mrs A. Bell, and the nine-year-old boy Dennis Gillingham. The Luftwaffe, however, had not quite finished with Yeovil and would come again once more in the late summer of 1942.

War Weapons Week, 1941

During the spring of 1941, 'War Weapons Weeks' were organised to raise money through national savings to help the war effort. Yeovil's War Weapons Week from Sunday 3 May to Saturday the 10th with the slogan 'Lend to Defend the Seas for the Free', set a target of £300,000, and after suffering air raids in which townspeople had been killed and wounded, Yeovilians were in the mood to meet, and if possible, exceed the target.

The week began at 3 p.m. on Saturday 3 May with a military parade and march-past through the town centre to the football ground at Huish while overhead several RAF fighter aircraft did victory rolls. Captain Harold Balfour MC, MP, under-secretary of state for air, officially opened the week with a stirring speech in which he proclaimed that the RAF bomber force would eventually cause the destruction of Germany and bring victory to this country; the enemy, he promised, would get bomb for bomb. However, no one listening at the Huish ground could foresee that it would take another four years to achieve the victory. As if to remind Yeovilians that the road would be long and hard, the air raid warning was sounded at 9.45 p.m. on that Saturday evening as enemy aircraft flew overhead on their way to and from targets in the north of England, and the all clear did not go until 4.20 a.m. the following morning.

The Saturday evening fundraising dance at Grass Royal school was cut short by the air raid warning.

Over 1,000 people gathered on the South Street car park on Sunday afternoon for a Drumhead Service followed by an inspection and parade of local civil defence and youth organisations. The Yeovil Temple Salvation Army band played, and a male voice choir from the army camp at Houndstone led the communal singing. That night, the air raid alert lasted for six hours.

In the Borough, still bearing the scars of the Good Friday bombing, a large indicator board was set up, and on each evening during the week, there was a target hour ceremony when the mayor displayed the amount raised that day and guest speakers would address the crowd.

Monday 5 May was 'Town Day' and the target hour ceremony announced the collection of £114,000. The overnight air raid alert lasted five hours.

Tuesday was 'Ladies' Day' and the guest of honour at the target hour ceremony was the Countess of Ilchester; the mayor announced that £144,300 had now been raised. The overnight alert went on for five hours.

Wednesday 7 May was 'Glovers' and Westland's Day' with fundraising in the town's factories, and the target hour ceremony announced income of over £190,000. The overnight alert lasted five and three-quarters hours, and a German bomber passing overhead fired down the beam of one of the local searchlights.

Thursday 8 May was 'Traders' Day' with a military band playing in the Borough during the afternoon, and a massed parade of firefighters was held in the evening. The funds announced at the target ceremony had reached nearly £200,000. During that night's five and a half hours alert, a lone German bomber struck and cut the cable of the Yew Tree Close barrage balloon and dropped its load of high explosive bombs. Several properties in area, including the RAF balloon crew's accommodation hut, were damaged by blast. Two of the bombs failed to explode and thankfully there were no casualties; the German bomber flew on undamaged and the barrage balloon floated away.

Friday, Yeovil Market day, was 'Farmers' and Country Day' and Saturday 10 May was 'Defence Services' Day.' At the last target hour ceremony, the mayor described the final two days' efforts as magnificent, and he announced that £164,600 had been raised making the grand total of £400,600, thus exceeding the town's target by £100,600.

The air raid alert on Friday 9 May lasted for three hours, but as if to give the weary Yeovilians a brief rest, the Saturday night alert lasted only half an hour.

During War Weapons Week, there were fundraising darts matches, luncheons, dances, fashion shows, sales of work, street savings groups, and a children's poster competition. Selling centres, staffed by volunteers, were set up in various places in the town centre and people seen not carrying their gas masks were challenged by ARP members and then 'fined', the proceeds going to buy national savings certificates.

The Yeovil 'Gas Attack'

In August 1941, despite the nation suffering heavy air raids, poison gas had not been unleashed, but with memories of its extensive use on the Western Front in the First World War, the fear remained that Nazi Germany might resort to this dreadful form of warfare.

On Friday, 8 August 1941, a notice appeared in the *Western Gazette* announcing that an intended tear gas exercise would be held on the following day in Yeovil town centre, but no time was given, other than it would happen between 2 p.m. and 6 p.m.

Reporting on 15 August, the *Gazette* stated that the local civil defence authorities had expressed themselves well satisfied with the public's reaction to the exercise, but they went on to comment that there were many indications that it could not be regarded as a reliable guide to the state of readiness in the event of a real poison gas attack. The public had been warned in advance, and therefore, there was a lack of genuine surprise, and possibly as a result, there seemed to be fewer people in the town than usual on a Saturday afternoon. The *Gazette* went on to say that although the advanced warning had given no precise time, there appeared to be many in the 'danger area' who obviously knew exactly the 'zero hour'.

Tear gas was released in the town centre in Silver Street, the Borough, and Princes Street, and the 'attack' lasted for about half an hour from the time the hand rattles sounded the warning until hand bells rang the 'all clear.' Air raid wardens and two first-aid teams were on duty, and six people who had either forgotten to carry their gas masks, or wore leaky ones, were treated for the effects of the tear gas. A loudspeaker car drove around the area telling people what to do and where to go for treatment. The civil defence observers were gratified to see that all passengers alighting from buses entering the 'danger area' were wearing their gas masks. However, the results of the exercise revealed several problems which the authorities would need to deal with including the performance of some of the civilian gas masks. Although the masks were reported to have stood up well to the test, the steaming up of the micah eyepieces made easy recognition of passers-by difficult, and some people were seen to be feeling their way cautiously around corners.

The *Western Gazette* reported that for a few days before the exercise many townspeople had visited the air raid precautions headquarters to have their gas masks tested or changed. One evacuee mother staying in the town, whose daughter would be coming to stay with her for the weekend, had borrowed a mask in case the girl forgot to bring her own.

Cigarettes were strictly rationed to one packet per person per purchase, but the *Gazette* reported that one sharp character had bought a packet of cigarettes in a shop, and when the warning was sounded, he had put on his mask and had gone back in so 'disguised' and bought a second packet. The *Western Gazette* was silent on its source.

A Military Tattoo and Tanks

Saturday, 13 September 1941 was the day chosen for the Military Daylight Tattoo presented by the resident royal artillery anti-aircraft unit at Lufton camp to give local people a glimpse of the life of an army recruit from the time of his call-up until his training was complete. The military camps had been established at Houndstone and Lufton just before the outbreak of the Second World War in the summer of 1939; Houndstone camp was on the east side of Boundary Road and Lufton on the west.

The free event commenced at 3 p.m. and to bring spectators to Lufton Camp, a bus service left Pen Mill station every fifteen minutes, calling at Town Station, the Triangle, the Borough, Red Lion hotel in Kingston, Westfield hotel, and Preston Pucknett.

Several hundred Yeovilians gathered at the camp and the tattoo began with an 'awkward squad' of recruits being given their first drills and with insights into the methods of training, which in the words of the *Western Gazette* would give them 'the confidence and bearing of the best type of British soldier'. The later phases of training were presented by men who had been in the army for five weeks. A battery march-past by men with only three weeks of training, led by Second Lieutenant W. Widdupp, MM, gave an exhibition of parade-ground discipline. This was followed by glimpses of life in the field with trainee cooks of seven weeks of experience demonstrating cooking under combat conditions.

An exhibition of air co-operation with ground troops was given, during which several aircraft flew low over the troops and 'bombed' them with cigarettes. Junior instructors of the anti-aircraft battery gave a gunnery display and demonstrated the predictor described as 'an amazing invention which sights the guns by remote power and predicts the course of the 'plane without human assistance'. The displays were interspersed with physical training routines and the regimental band played throughout the afternoon.

Shortly after the tattoo, a column of Matilda and Valentine tanks arrived in Yeovil and were welcomed by the mayor, Councillor S. Duckworth, who said that their presence was to help make townspeople 'Tank conscious' and stimulate the war savings campaign. The column was touring the country under the command of Lt H. F. Turpin who had been chosen by the Ministry of Supply for this propaganda campaign because of his experience of action in the early stages of the war. The lieutenant gave the townspeople gathered around his tanks a vivid account of how the British tanks had been outnumbered 'by hordes of German tanks', which had swept through France and Belgium and eventually resulted in the evacuation from Dunkirk. He went on to stress that this would not happen again if everyone played their part and invested all they could spare in war savings.

In reporting the visit, the *Yeovil Review* also told readers of the splendid effort of the Pen Mill School savings groups had made to raise £374 in ten weeks to provide ten tommy guns. The 'baby class' had raised enough to buy one of the tommy guns.

Around the Town in 1941

German Oil

On 14 February 1941, the *Western Gazette* reported on a talk given by an official of the Ministry of Information to Yeovil rotary club about Germany's search for oil. The speaker said:

> Germany was today in possession of the Roumanian [*sic.*] oil fields, but to make use of oil from that source she had to transport it through the bottle-neck of the Danube, and it could not help her very much this year. But it could help Germany if she decided on a campaign in the Middle East. It was quite possible that Germany would attempt to seize the oil wells in Irak [*sic.*] and Iran. Mr Hugh Dalton (President of the Board of Trade) had said that existing German stocks of oil were being continually drawn upon, and were exposed to air attack. It was estimated that Germany's oil stocks would last for two years if she did not embark upon a major campaign. If she started a 'blitz' on a huge scale, then Germany would have to draw very deeply on her reserves

and could not afford a second 'blitz'. Britain controlled 20 per cent of the oil resources of the world, and so long as we commanded the seas, then we had ample supplies of all the oil products we needed. America was the biggest oil power in the world, and her co-operation would mean that Germany had not a chance of getting the oil that was so valuable to her.

Five months later, on 22 June 1941, Germany launched a 'second blitz' and invaded Russia, and the rest, as they say, is history.

The Sundial Railings

The railings around the sundial in Sidney Gardens erected in 1912 by the borough council to commemorate Mr Sidney Watts's gift of the gardens to the town were taken away in 1941 for the war effort and never replaced. However, the sundial managed to survive relatively unscathed for some fifty-five years without them until the sundial was removed following its partial demolition by unknown vandals.

Tommy Guns

On 3 October 1941, the *Western Gazette* reported:

In the Summer Savings Campaign the Pen Mill School Savings Group which embraces Yeovil children and their relations, and children from the Christchurch Church of England School, Southwark, has saved in the ten weeks ending September 30th, £374 for sub-machine 'Tommy' guns for the Army. The target for the ten weeks was £300 which will provide 10 of these weapons. The baby class, which has a 100 per cent membership, has alone provided money for one gun. One child became a member of the group when it was only two days old. Since January 1941, over £1,400 has been saved in the school group which now has 470 members and much credit for this achievement is due to the Hon. Secretary of the Group, Miss Beel of the School teaching staff.

'See Munitions Being Made for One Week'

The *Western Gazette* reported:

From December 13 to 20th at Vincent's Showroom, Princes Street, Yeovil you can see girls from a West Country factory actively making parts of air-craft before your eyes. They do the jobs just as they do them at the factory—you can see how easily they do the skilled work, and how simple other operations are. If you don't know what factory work is like, here's your chance to find out. Wander round, talk to the girls, ask all the questions you like. It's not a matter of enrolling for war-work—unless you want to, of course, in which case there will be somebody who can tell you all about the jobs going. But nobody will take your name or address unless you wish. So drop in at this War Job Bureau during the week. You'll be sorry if you miss.

Wartime censorship would not allow the name of the factory to be given, but it was of course the Westland Aircraft Works.

The Romance of Poisons

The weekly luncheon of the Yeovil Rotary club on 2 December, was followed by a talk entitled 'The Romance of Poisons' by Mr F. P. Pendray, who pointed out the considerable interest of the general public in the study of poisons and poisoners. Mr Pendray explained the use of poisons, the tolerance of people and animals to them, and the knowledge of poisons by the Greeks, Romans, and Early Saxons and by pathologists and toxicologists of modern times.

The 'Poor Box'

In December, the *Yeovil Review* told the story of how the present 'poor box' at the Yeovil magistrates' court came into existence:

It was really due to a minor motoring offence committed a few months ago by Mr. A.C. Baynes, of London, who is none other than the famous radio star—Stainless Stephen. Unable to appear in court in answer to the summons he sent £1 with a request that if the fine should be less, the balance should be placed in the poor box.

He was fined 10/-, and the poor box, which had been non-existent for a long number of years again came into being with a donation of 10/- which has since been added to by further contributions which has enabled the court to assist those unfortunate victims of circumstances, which occasionally come before them. Thanks to Stainless Stephen—that's how the poor box came to be started.

Above: The parade of veterans and war widows marching through Yeovil on Peace Day, 19 July 1919.

Right: The author's father, Reginald Sweet MM, served in Yeovil as an air raid warden during the whole of the war.

The Yeovil Roll of Honour.

High Street in 1938.

Westland Works viewed from West Coker Road in the mid-1930s.

NCOs stationed at Houndstone camp in 1939.

Officers and ratings of No. 1 Flying School at RNAS Yeovilton.

Opposite above: Mr Herbert Morrison, MP, shakes the hand of the carnival queen at the Huish football ground.

Opposite below: A Westland Lysander on Westland's airfield.

A postcard sent in March 1941.

All the evacuees arrived at Yeovil town station.

A postcard sent on 4 September 1939, the day after war was declared with the following message: 'Here I am today at Yeovil, such a lot of children arrived. How dreadful the war, but I thought it would happen'.

Barrage balloons.

One of the heavy rescue teams.

Members of the Women's Auxiliary Air Force (WAAFs), who operated the barrage balloon at Bunford Hollow.

Princes Street from Bide's Gardens, Yeovil

The captured German gun points menacingly towards Princes Street.

The grave in Yeovil Cemetery of the three unknown victims of the air raid on 8 October.

Opposite above: Members of the Yeovil home guard company parade on Southville.

Opposite below: Communal air raid shelters at the rear of Goldcroft, photographed in 2004.

Guaranteed Circulation 5000 Copies

REVIEW
YEOVIL

Vol. 4, Part 10.　　　　　JULY, 1940.

GRATIS WHEN DELIVERED.
EXTRA COPIES 1d

Printed and Published by the Proprietors, EDWIN SNELL & SONS, Park Road, Yeovil.　Telephone **24.**

The front cover of the *Yeovil Review* of July 1940.

The 18-hp Austin Yeovil war-time town ambulance.

The Yeovil fire brigade's fire escape unit and crew.

Above: The guard of honour accompanying the coffin of patrol officer Charles Gillard along Kingston to Yeovil Cemetery.

Opposite: Pages from the borough air raid siren logbook showing the warnings sounded in May and part of June 1941.

MAY. 1941.

Thurs 1ᵉ 9. 55pm to 1.15 am
Fri 2ᵈ 10. 30pm to 11.20 pm
Sat 3ᵈ 9. 45pm to 4.30 am
Sun 4ᵉ 8. 45am to 9am
- 4ᵉ 11. 10pm to 5.5 am
Mon 5ᵗ 11. 50pm to 4.50 am
Tues 6ᵗ 11. 40pm to 4.45 am
Wed 7ᵗ 11. 15pm to 5 am
Thurs 8ᵗ 11. 45pm to 3. 30 am
(bombs on Yeovil - Headford Rd)
Fri 9ᵗ 11. 15pm to 2.15 am
Sat 10ᵗ 12. 10pm to 12.40 pm
Sun 11ᵗ 12. 15 am to 12.40 am
- 11ᵗ 8. 15 pm to 10pm
- 11ᵗ 11. 30pm to 5 am
(bombs on Yeovilton)
Wed 14ᵗ 5. 30pm to 6.30p
Fri 16ᵗ 12 30 am to 1.30am
- 16ᵗ 12 night to 3 am
@(bombs on Hedford Rd)
Sun 18ᵗ 4. 15 am to 4.40 am

MAY (Contᵈ)

Wed 21ᵗ 12. 15 am to 1 am
- 21ᵗ 1 pm to 1.10pm
Sat 24ᵗ 11. 55 pm to 12. 25p
(bombs on Hedford Rd)
Mon 26ᵗ 11. 35 am to 11. 45 a
- 26ᵗ 1. 40 pm to 2. 55p
Thurs 29ᵗ 12. 10 am to 1.10am
- 29ᵗ 2. 5 am to 4. 10 am
Fri 30ᵗ 7. 30pm to 8. 30p
Sat 31ˢᵗ 12. 30 am to 4. 10
- 31ˢᵗ 10. 30 am to 11 am
- 31ˢᵗ 11. 55 pm to 4 am

JUNE. 1941.

Sun 1ˢᵗ 12 night to 3. 55a
Wed 4ᵗ 2. 5 am to 2. 15a
Thurs 5ᵗ 12. 5 am to 3. 55
Sat 7ᵗ 12. 5 am to 12. 35
Mon 9ᵗ 12. 20 am to 1 am
- 9ᵗ 2. 20 pm to 3.10 p
Tues 10ᵗ 1. 15 am to 1. 30
Wed 11ᵗ 6. 55 pm to 7. 30

IMPORTANT NOTICE,

A TEAR GAS EXERCISE

WILL BE HELD (if weather conditions permit) in

YEOVIL

ON

SATURDAY, AUGUST 9th, 1941

at some time between 1 p.m. and 8 p.m.
(for about HALF AN HOUR)

The objects of the EXERCISE are :

(1) To accustom the public to gas signals; i.e. the Rattles indicate the presence of gas and the Handbells the " All Clear "

(2) To practice the public in obtaining protection against gas.

(3) To test the fit of respirators.

The TEAR GAS to be used is HARMLESS, but will cause smarting of the eyes unless respirators are worn.

CARRY YOUR GAS MASK AND BE PREPARED TO WEAR IT.

ADVICE

As soon as the Rattles sound :

(1) Put on your respirator.

(2) Take young children into shops or houses.

(3) Cover any food to keep the gas off it

(4) Shut all doors and windows.

(5) If you get gas into your eyes, consult a Warden or Policeman who will direct you where to go for treatment ; if facilities available, bathe the eye in a normal saline solution, one teaspoonful of salt to a pint of boiled (not boiling) water.

(6) If exposed to a heavy concentration of the harmless gas, your clothes may give off some gas if you approach a fire after the exercise.

A. S KEEP, M.C (CAPT.)
Area Organiser.

The advertisement giving notice of the 'Gas Attack'.

Above: Officers and men of an anti-aircraft battery serving at Houndstone camp.

Right: The star of '6 HAPPY DAYS' at the Odeon cinema.

Deanna Durbin

Left: 'WRENS' (Women's Royal Naval Service) at RNAS Yeovilton in 1942.

Below: Barwick House was the HQ of several US Army replacement battalions.

BARWICK HOUSE

THE SIGNAL IS
SAVE

THE NAVY'S HERE
Lend more power to their elbow.
Save every shilling you can to help
pay for the ships and guns they need
to smash the enemy and to guard
our Merchant Fleet.

IT'S WARSHIP WEEK
This is your special chance to Save
and Lend for Victory. Think what
you owe to the Navy. Make your
money fight under the White Ensign.
WAR SAVINGS ARE WARSHIPS

Right: A poster advertising
'Warship Week'.

Below: A Churchill Tank (Mk VII).

CHURCHILL MARK VII

Sidney Gardens was a popular venue for 'Holidays at Home'.

Bomb-damaged houses in Gordon Road. (*National Archives*)

The Westland Whirlwind twin-engine fighter-bomber.

Seafires and Spitfires under construction at Westland Works.

Above: Checking books from the 'Book Recovery Drive'.

Left: The company band leads the Yeovil Borough company home guard through High Street in the parade on the opening day of the 'Wings for Victory Week'.

An ENSA programme.

Air raid wardens of the West Coker Road wardens' post.

Staff of the Yeovil fire guard office.

Lieutenant Alec George Horwood, VC, DCM.

Advertisements for 'Salute the Solder Week'.

Observers serving at the Royal Observer Corps' group centre in Southwoods.

A V-1 flying bomb at the Imperial War Museum, Duxford.

Above: The fire at the Manor Hotel was quickly brought under control.

Right: A United States GI celebrates VE-Day over the entrance to Donut Dugout at the Newnam Hall.

Crowds celebrating VE-Day in the Borough.

Female members of the Royal Observer Corps march in the parade to the Huish football ground for the public Thanksgiving service on 9 May. In the foreground, some American GIs watch the parade.

Three cheers for the peace at the Orchard Street VJ-Day party.

Residents of the Orchard Street Victory outing, enjoying the lunch stop on Abbotsbury Hill.

MEREDITH WE'RE OUT!

DEMOBILISATION CENTRE

OUT

Kiss me Searg. !! "
(or famous last words.)

Above: Carols were sung in St John's Church on the first Christmas Day of peace. The tracery of two windows in the south elevation still show signs of bomb damage from the air raid on 12 October 1941.

Left: 'Goodbye!' The war is over.

The War Memorial Yeovil

Yeovil Borough war memorial.

Preston Plucknett war memorial.

At the Odeon

'6 HAPPY DAYS with DEANNA DURBIN' at the Odeon Cinema in Court Ash began on Monday 1 December with a different film every day:

Monday	*3 Smart Girls.*
Tuesday	*100 Men and a Girl.*
Wednesday	*Mad about Music.*
Thursday	*That Certain Age.*
Friday	*3 Smart Girls Grow Up.*
Saturday	*First Love.*

6

1942

Some Important Events

From January	United States Army and from May the United States Army Air Corps begin to arrive in Great Britain.
15 January	Japanese invade Burma (Myanmar).
15 February	Japanese capture Singapore.
4 June	United States naval victory at Midway Island in the Pacific.
1 July	Basic civilian petrol ration abolished. Petrol only available for official users. Nearly all foodstuffs now rationed apart from game, fish, vegetables, and bread.
23 October	Battle of El Alamein begins.
8 November	Operation Torch—Allies invade North-West Africa.
16 November	German 6th Army surrounded at Stalingrad.

The Americans Are Over Here

Following the entry of the United States of America into the war, the south-west of England was designated as the area from which the United States Army would launch their part in the invasion of occupied Europe when it came. From early in 1942, through 1943 and 1944, tens of thousands of United States servicemen and women, infantry, artillery, armour, airborne infantry, engineers, support units, and the US Army Air Corps poured into the western counties. Camps sprang up, depots were established, hospitals were built (until recently former US hospital buildings at Bristol Frenchay and Musgrove Park hospital in Taunton were still being used), and the myriad of other facilities needed to service an army were constructed. Ken Wakefield's book *Operation Bolero* published by Crecy Books in 1994 gives a first-class account of the Americans in Bristol and the west country from 1942–45.

The influx of large numbers of troops of any nationality can be the cause of friction between rival units, national forces, and the civilian population; the arrival of the American GIs in the area was no exception. However, the three years the 'Yanks' were here seemed to have passed off reasonably well.

In and around Yeovil, the US Army set up the 121st and 169th General Hospitals at Lufton and Houndstone camps as well as a large engineer unit at Houndstone. Supply depots dotted the area, and on Barwick Park, a large camp of Quonset huts (the American version of the Nissen hut) and tents was established for several replacement battalions.

Yeovilians who lived through those momentous years will have memories of the Americans who filled the roads with their jeeps, large lorries and transporters, all with the white star prominent on the olive-green drab camouflage. The smartly dressed GIs were everywhere—in the cinemas, pubs, and at dances; they provided a stark contrast to the drabness of wartime Britain. The endless informal games of base-ball played out wherever there was space, youngsters 'ambushing' the GIs for chewing gum, 'any gum chum' and candy, all so readily given. The colourful and exciting 'American Comics' with Superman, Batman, and other heroes, the possession of which was worth more than gold.

In March 1944, two ladies working for the American Red Cross came to Yeovil with instructions to set up a club for US servicemen stationed in and around the town. They were Miss Lois Latham from North Carolina and Miss Amy P. Lang, who hailed from Massachusetts. Within three days of their arrival, they had found a small empty shop in the town centre and were soon serving coffee and donuts to queues of American GIs.

All across England, the American Red Cross was opening Donut Dugout clubs, where the GIs could enjoy coffee, donuts, and other refreshments in a service club atmosphere. Lois and Amy soon obtained the use of South Street Baptist Church, Newnam Memorial Hall (now Pegasus Court), and transformed it into a Donut Dugout fully equipped Class 'A' US servicemen's club.

Interviewed by a *Western Gazette* reporter in February 1945, Miss Latham described the beginning and working of the club both for the welfare and comfort of the GIs, and how the pair had come to 'love Yeovil and Somerset' during their time in the town. The smell of hot donuts from Donut Dugout in the Newnam Memorial Hall is one that stays with the author over seventy-five years later.

The build-up of troops and vehicles of all descriptions during the late spring of 1944, filling the roads and streets, was the sign that something big was coming; suddenly, they were gone as it was D-Day—6 June.

There may be some 'old Yeovilians' who can still remember the Saturday morning four days later on 10 June 1944, when to quote the *Western Gazette*:

> Over 1,500 members of the Children's Club were present at the Odeon Cinema on Saturday when a U.S. Army Band gave a special Programme consisting of martial and swing music, tap-dancing, hillbilly turns &c. The Resident Manager, Mr. Ronald F. Hart, introducing the players said they would remember the kindness and generosity of American troops in this country for a long time.

Following the invasion, the United States forces were gradually reduced and by the end of 1945 they had gone from Yeovil, Donut Dugout had closed, but an indelible memory would still remain.

On Sunday, 5 December 2004, a ceremony was held in the Borough dedicating a plaque placed on the wall of Lloyds bank in honour of the US troops stationed in and around Yeovil during the time leading up to D-Day and to the end of the war. The plaque was unveiled by United States Air Force Colonel Gildner of the United States Embassy, followed by a wreath-laying at the war memorial. The site was felt to be the right place for the commemorative plaque as the US Army collected the wages for the local troops from the Bank.

ERECTED BY THE PEOPLE OF YEOVIL
IN GRATEFUL COMMEMORATION OF
THE AMERICAN TROOPS WHO WERE
STATIONED IN AND AROUND OUR TOWN
PRIOR TO THE D-DAY LANDINGS ON
6 JUNE 1944 MANY OF WHOM
SACRIFICED THEIR LIVES
IN THE CAUSE OF FREEDOM
6 JUNE 2004

Warship Week, 1942

During the Second World War, the National Savings movement conducted campaigns to raise money for the war effort, one of which was 'Warship Week' running from October 1941 to March 1942, and local savings committees fixed their week during this period. Yeovil and District's Week would begin on Saturday, 28 February 1942 and finish the following Saturday, on 7 March.

The local target was £300,000, the cost of building a destroyer for the Royal Navy; raising this sum would allow the Yeovil district to 'adopt' the destroyer HMS *Hesperus*. The money would be raised by a variety of means and a programme of events.

Warship Week began with the formal opening of the war savings bureau at 2 High Street, followed by a march-past through the town to the Huish football ground of contingents of the fighting services led by five bands. Present were the Royal Navy, the Fleet Air Arm, Royal Artillery with heavy and light anti-aircraft guns, 11th Battalion West Yorkshire regiment riding in bren gun carriers, the RAF, the Yeovil Borough Company home guard, and the three women's services: the WRNS, ATS, and WAAF. As the parade marched past King George Street, the salute was taken by the mayor, Councillor S. Duckworth, standing by the archway indicator which would show the daily and overall amounts saved during the week.

At the Huish ground, Commander Sir Archibald Southby, MP, formally opened Warship Week and several fighter aircraft swooped down over the town to give force to Sir Archibald's appeal for more air and sea power to meet the immediate needs of the Allies now fighting Nazi Germany and Japan.

All day Saturday, 'The Mystery Man' roamed the town centre giving prizes of savings stamps. His photograph was placed in shop windows, and successful challengers had to be carrying a programme of the week's events and say 'You are the Mystery Man. I claim the Yeovil Warship Prize'. The 'Mystery Man' also left cards at various places and finders could claim savings stamps from the savings bureau.

On Saturday evening, the Yeovil Philharmonic Society gave a concert in the Park School hall, organised by the Baptist Fellowship, and there were dances at Grass Royal and Summerleaze Park schools.

On Sunday afternoon, 1 March, the Band of the Royal Marines gave a concert in the Gaumont Cinema. A naval, military, aircraft and Air Force exhibition, organised by the Royal Observer Corps opened on Monday morning in the Liberal Club and included equipment from downed German aircraft. Monday evening saw the Yeovil Squadron Air Training Corps giving a display of gymnastics and boxing at Grass Royal school.

The South Petherton Musical Society began a three-evening run of Gilbert and Sullivan's *The Gondoliers* on Monday at Summerleaze Park school, and at the same time, heats in the 'Ankle' competitions opened at the Odeon and Gaumont cinemas. The grand final was held a week later with Miss Hussey the winner at the Odeon, and Miss E. J. Batchelor taking the prize at the Gaumont.

On Tuesday evening, a grand Beetle drive, organised by the lady telephonists, was held in the fire station, and leading fireman Trask played the piano during the interval. The Yeovil and District Young Farmers club gave a dance at Grass Royal school with an RAF band providing the music for the 130 dancers.

On Wednesday afternoon, the Comic Dog Show held in Messrs W. Palmer & Co.'s market attracted seventy-nine entries and raised £18. An exhibition of tricks was given by 'Garcon' a white poodle owned by Miss Higson of Lufton Manor. During the evening, the Yeovil Literary and Dramatic Society presented a 'War Time Variety Concert and Play'.

One of the highlights of Thursday was the afternoon Baby Show in the Park School hall. There were 168 entries in eight classes of which seventy babies were entered in the class for the best all-round baby. The national fire brigade presented a firefighting display during the afternoon at the Huish football ground and there was a display of aerobatics over the town by a couple of fighter aircraft.

A naval aquatic sports exhibition of swimming and diving was organised by personnel from RNAS Yeovilton in the Huish swimming pool during Thursday evening. The RAF radio show 'Out of the Blue' was presented at Grass Royal school to a sell-out audience, with many standing. The all-professional artistes included Johnny Lockwood, described as 'Tommy Handley's Stooge'. For those readers under a certain age, ask your gran or grandad who Tommy Handley was. Members of the audience who bought a 2s 6d savings stamp were given a cigarette—a much-treasured gift at a time when cigarettes were scarce. The Royal Observer Corps' Thursday evening dance in the Assembly Rooms to Al Lever's Band from Weston-super-Mare raised £100 from the 480 dancers.

Yeovil 'B' Company of the home guard organised a concert and dance at the Southville drill hall on Friday evening. Music for dancing was provided by the Royal Army Service Corps Band and Mr Pittard's concert party entertained. The Yeovil Youth Movement held an 'Under Twenties' dance at Grass Royal school and over 200 youngsters danced to the RAF band. During the interval, Lt-Cdr Count Metax told sea stories.

Saturday 7 March was designated 'Children's Day' and well over 1,500 children accompanied by their schoolteachers attended the morning film show in the Odeon. In addition to the films, which included a Ministry of Information film and one on national savings, there were songs by the joint choirs of Summerleaze Park and Grass Royal schools, folk dancers in costume, piano and accordion solos, an instrumental quartet and children of the Westland Pantomime Company presented the fairy scene from *Dick Whittington*. A football match in the afternoon between a Yeovil team and a RAF side at the Huish ground resulted in the Yeovilians winning 6–2. 'Warship Week' ended with dances at Summerleaze Park school organised by the Royal Observer Corps, and at Grass Royal school arranged by the Yeovil fire service.

During the week, factories, shops, and offices in the town and district held collections; the final sum raised from all sources was over £425,000, which exceeded the target by £125,000, and the people 'adopted' the destroyer HMS *Hesperus*. The ensign of the destroyer was laid up in St John's Church in January 1946 following her decommissioning at the end of the war. Built by Thorneycroft at Southampton in 1939, HMS *Hesperus* was destined for the Brazilian Navy under the name *Juruena,* but on the outbreak of war in September 1939, the destroyer was requisitioned by the Royal Navy and named *Hesperus* after the Greek Evening Star. With a displacement of 1,400 tons, the *Hesperus* had a complement of 145 officers and men, and her armament consisted of three 4.7-inch guns, one 3-inch AA gun, and four 21-inch torpedo tubes; later, one of the guns was replaced by hedgehog depth-charge projectors.

The *Hesperus* served most of the war in the North Atlantic where she was engaged on convoy escort duty. The role of the escort was vitally important in keeping the nation's supply lines open against German U-boat attacks. It was a long, tedious, and very unpleasant task battling with the North Atlantic, often in fearsome conditions and with the constant fear of U-boat attack. However, the *Hesperus* was a successful ship, and on convoy duty and in anti-submarine sweeps, she sank five U-boats and damaged several others. In one action, the destroyer brought the German *U-357* to the surface by depth charge attack and then sank the enemy submarine by ramming it. The battle honours awarded to HMS *Hesperus* were Norway, 1940; Atlantic 1940–45; and English Channel, 1945.

In October 1993, a civic service of remembrance and dedication for the crew of the *Hesperus* was held at St John's Church followed by a parade and march-past.

Buy a Tank

On 20 July 1942, national savings opened a ten-week campaign to increase the amount of small savings by 20 per cent over the sums collected in 1941. The objective of the campaign was the purchase of battle tanks, and the War Office would allow the names of the towns or counties who were successful in reaching the 20 per cent target or more to be inscribed on a tank. The larger the increase, the heavier the tank to bear the place name. If the 20 per cent target was reached, Yeovil would have two light tanks named 'Yeovil', 25 per cent two medium tanks, and if 30 per cent or more was achieved, two heavy Churchill tanks would bear the town's name.

The campaign under the slogan of 'TANKS FOR ATTACK' would target the small savings groups of streets, schools, and factories. The target for Yeovil was £91,150, but the early returns were very disappointing. The savings were not coming in due, in the organisers' opinions, to the August holiday period, but then the zeal and energy of the 300 group secretaries in Yeovil began to bear fruit, and the town exceeded its target with total savings of £98,612. Throughout the ten weeks of the campaign, a savings bureau had been open in High Street, voluntarily staffed by ladies of the Yeovil Inner Wheel, and nearly £11,000 was invested through the bureau. With the target well exceeded, Yeovil would get its name on two Churchill tanks.

The town had also met all the target figures for previous national savings campaigns—War Weapons Week in 1941, War Ship Week earlier in 1942, and now in Tanks for Attack—raising nearly £1,000,000, through, in the words of the *Yeovil Review*, 'the untiring energy and enthusiastic army of workers and the great body of patriotic townspeople.'

Six of the town's savings groups who had the best results were also to have their names inscribed on tanks—Westland, Highfield Road, St Michaels' Avenue, Cedar Grove, Orchard Street, and Glenthorne Avenue. It is not known whether the names were inscribed and if so, what happened to the tanks.

On 8 April 1944, the *Western Gazette* reported that a letter had been received by the Yeovil and district national savings committee from Lt

Peter Ormrod, Scots Guards, Royal Tank Corps, stating that he had in his detachment a heavy fighting vehicle presented by Yeovil as a result of the 1942 'Tanks for Attack' campaign. Lt Ormrod wrote in the *Western Gazette*:

> It is crewed by L/Sgt Moss, L/Corp Gliddon, and Guardsmen Pirie, Forbes and Burke, who tell me that this is the best running vehicle in the detachment. I wonder if you would like to adopt this vehicle and also suggest a suitable name? I feel sure we will have the thoughts and support of the subscribers to this vehicle in our efforts to free the world from the Nazis tyranny in the coming battle.

The committee agreed to adopt the tank and named it 'The Yeovilian', and also to extend the *'Hesperus'* fund to include 'The Yeovilian's' crew (plus any further adopted units) and to immediately send a parcel of cigarettes and 10 shillings to each member of the tank crew with the committee's good wishes.

On 8 June 1945, the *Western Gazette* reported:

> News of Yeovil's own tank, 'The Yeovilian' has been received by Mr E. A. Stagg, hon. secretary to Yeovil Savings Committee.
>
> The tank, one of the latest model Churchills designed to co-operate with infantry against strongly defended positions, was in a battalion of the Scots Guards in the 6th Guards Armoured Brigade which fought its way from the Normandy Beaches to Lubeck on the shores of the Baltic. They were constantly in action, and fought with Scottish, British and Airborne Infantry, also on several occasions with American infantry and airborne troops.
>
> The 'Yeovilian' is known to have survived the battles of Normandy, but her ultimate progress has been difficult to ascertain. She has, however, more than played her part in winning the victory.

In August 1942

During the first week of August, we had been at war with Nazi Germany for nearly three years, and there was no end in sight. However, despite the difficulties and worries of the time, Yeovilians carried on as best they could.

The cinemas were doing their part in keeping spirits up with *The Big Fella* at the Central Cinema; *A Night in New Orleans* and *These Kids from Town* at the Odeon; and down at the Gaumont in the Triangle, Tommy Trinder was starring in *The Foreman Went to France*. The national savings committee's mobile cinema talent spotting competition 'Let the Children Sing' held its grand final in the Borough on Saturday morning 1 August.

During 1942, the opportunity for holidays away from home could be quite limited, and 'Home Holidays' was a national scheme to provide entertainment for the many people who could not get away because of the difficulties in travelling and the closure or restriction of holiday beaches and resorts. Here in Yeovil, the town's home holidays ran for a month from mid-July to 16 August, and during the first week of August, the local organisers had arranged a variety of events beginning on Saturday afternoon with a children's fancy dress parade from Sidney Gardens to the Huish football ground, followed by children's sports. On Saturday evening, there was a dance at Grass Royal school organised by the Air Raid Precautions Social Committee with dancing to the Westland Dance Orchestra, and over 200 danced to the Blackmore Vale Orchestra at the Wessex Electricity company's evening dance at Summerleaze Park school. On Sunday 2 August, the band of the Czech Forces gave an afternoon concert in Sidney Gardens.

August Bank Holiday Monday saw a full programme, with an open athletics meeting at the Westland sports ground, and the Wessex Electricity company's cricket match and athletics meeting with side shows was held on the Mudford Road playing fields. An evening's open-air dance followed at the playing fields, and another dance was organised by Wessex Electricity at Summerleaze Park school with dancing to Mons. Paquay and his Band.

On Tuesday evening, over 400 people packed into the public swimming baths in Huish to enjoy an inter-service swimming gala, which included a demonstration by the local military of transporting wounded soldiers across rivers and how to jump into water fully equipped from a height of 20 feet and swim 60 yards. Grass Royal school was crowded for an ENSA (entertainments national service association) concert with a cabaret show accompanied by Billy Kelly and his Westland Dance Orchestra.

At 9.10 p.m. on Wednesday evening, the air raid warning wailed, and four minutes later, two German Focke-Wulf (FW) 190 single-engined fighter-bombers flew low across the town with guns blazing.

Spirits had to be kept up, and the pages of the *Gazette* continued to cheerfully report on the events of home holidays week, with more concerts, dances, and sports taking up several columns of the 7 August edition. Looking back through these columns, the headlines 'YEOVIL HOLIDAY EVENTS BIG CROWDS AT ENTERTAINMENTS' mask the horror and fear of those few minutes past nine on that Wednesday evening in August 1942.

The Tenth and Last Air Raid

On Wednesday 5 August, beginning at 7.30 p.m. in Sidney Gardens, a large audience enjoyed an evening of entertainment with the Yeovil national fire service concert party, but by 9 p.m., the concert was over, the chairs packed away, and apart from a few people enjoying the late warm summer evening in the gardens, the audience had gone home or into town.

At 9.10 p.m., the air raid warning wailed—the 268th since the war began—and four minutes later, two German FW 190 single-engined fighter-bombers roared out of the east and flew at rooftop level across the town. With cannons and machine guns blazing, each aircraft dropped one 500-kg bomb then left.

One bomb exploded in the gardens at the rear of numbers 13, 14, and 15 Gordon Road and 2–8 (even) Grass Royal making a crater 9 m wide by 2 m deep, demolishing two of the houses in Gordon Road and leaving others badly damaged. Two brick-built reinforced-surface air raid shelters standing within 45 feet of the centre of the bomb crater were reported to have stood up well to the explosion with no signs of roof movement or displacement of walls and only some surface fragmentation damage. The second bomb struck the ground behind the Southville Salvation Army Temple, bounced into the air over Eastland Road and the leather dressing factory, and exploded in Dampier Street some 200 yards away. The shrapnel marks from this explosion can be still seen on the east wall of the Yeovil Centre off Reckleford.

When the all clear sounded half an hour later, thirty-eight years old George Mitchell had died from multiple wounds in his garden at 8 Grass Royal, and a critically injured First World War veteran Albert Hussey of 16 Gordon Road had been taken to Yeovil hospital but would die shortly after admission. In addition to the deaths of George Mitchell and Albert Hussey, twenty-six men, women, and children had been injured, ten seriously and tragically, after being rescued from her house at 6 Dampier Street, Miss Elsie Farwell would lose her fight for life on the following day, bringing the final death toll to three. The 'hit and run' raid also left fifteen houses destroyed or damaged beyond repair, and over 970 damaged.

Wartime censorship would only permit bare details of air raids to be reported, and on Friday 7 August 1942, the *Western Gazette* wrote:

Two German fighter-bombers, flying a little above house-top height, bombed and machine-gunned a West Country town in daylight on Wednesday evening. High explosives did damage to property in a residential area. There were some casualties, including one or two fatal.

The early morning air raid precautions tear gas exercise arranged for the 6 August in the Preston area was cancelled. The *Western Gazette* of Friday, 14 August 1942 reported:

The funeral took place on Monday of Miss Elsie Farwell, who died last week aged 59. She had been a member of the Salvation Army for over forty years being particularly associated with the Young People's Corps at Yeovil and had held the position of Record Sergeant for many years.

The funeral took place on Saturday of Mr. Albert George Mitchell, elder son of Mr. and Mrs. A. Mitchell, 17 Cromwell Road whose death occurred at the age of 38. A clerk at Messrs. W.J. & E.G. Ricketts & Company's glove factory, he was also a member of the Royal Observer Corps, and had been connected with St. Michael's Church and the Yeovil Parish Church. He was married and leaves a wife and an eight-year-old son.

The funeral took place at Yeovil Cemetery of Mr. Albert Victor Hussey, aged 46, a native of the town. He had been employed at the Corporation Gasworks as a van driver for 18 years and he had been a member of the Home Guard for about 12 months, having had previous military experience in the last war, when he served for three years with the Dorset Regiment in France. He was a member of the Yeovil Branch of the British Legion. Married twice, his second wife and a daughter survive him.

The air raid on the 5 August was the last time that bombs would fall on Yeovil.

Neither pilot of the two attacking FW 190s would survive the war; *Feldwebel* Karl Blasewere was shot down by RAF fighters near Start Point on 26 January 1943, and *Unteroffizier* Kurt Bressler would be downed by the RAF off Exmouth the following month, on 26 February.

Around the Town in 1942

Westland Workers' Panto

Beginning on 3 January and for ten days during the rest of the month, the Westland workers' pantomime *Dick Whittington* played to packed audiences in the company's sports pavilion off Westbourne Grove and at the school halls of Grass Royal and Summerleaze Park. The *Western Gazette* wrote:

> The colourful and jolly production scored a hit with many popular songs and amusing references to local places and Works celebrities. Two of the four scenes are laid in Middle Street and Ham Hill and the Cat has a war-time name 'Spitfire' and British markings on the back.

All proceeds from the show were shared between local charities.

The Spitfire/Whirlwind Fund

In September 1940, the 'Spitfire Fund' was launched in the town to raise £5,000 for the 'purchase' of a Spitfire, and by December, the fund had reached £4,200. On 14 February 1942, the *Western Gazette* reported that the fund had been renamed the 'Whirlwind Fund' in recognition of the Yeovil-built Westland Whirlwind fighter-bomber, and the target of £5,000 had been achieved.

Whirlwind number P7056—named 'The Pride of Yeovil'—had entered squadron service with the RAF in October 1941, carrying out offensive patrols, providing cover on bombing raids, and attacking enemy shipping and communications. The aircraft had recently undergone a major refit and had returned to active service. The Westland Whirlwinds were withdrawn from squadron service at the end of 1943.

Red Squirrels

Early in August, the *Western Gazette* reflected the 'keep calm and carry on' spirit, when it reported that following hard work by local 'enthusiasts', a colony of red squirrels had been re-established in Ninesprings. Sadly, the red squirrels did not survive long in their new home.

A Central Kitchen

The education committee approved a scheme for building a central kitchen at Eastland Road to provide dinners for Yeovil elementary school children at six dining centres in the town. The hourly wage rate for kitchen maids would be 11.5 pence; cooks, one shilling and six pence; and assistant cooks, 3.5 pence.

Fire Guard Duty

On 7 August, the *Western Gazette* reported that men not already engaged on fire guard duty, or other part-time national service, would soon be enrolled under a new compulsory order to carry out fire guard duties, and in the coming week, the government would make an order requiring fire guard training to be compulsory. All men born in the first half of 1924 were required to register for military service before the end of August.

The British Restaurant

Early in the war, with the introduction of strict food rationing, the government encouraged local authorities to establish publicly run British restaurants to provide nutritious and inexpensive hot meals. In the autumn of 1941, the borough council decided to open and manage a British restaurant in the Liberal Club in Middle Street, but problems with acquiring suitable equipment and appointing a suitable catering manager delayed the opening until 1 December 1942.

Mrs D. Trump, from Newport, Monmouthshire, was the first and only manageress of the restaurant, which provided accommodation for 200 diners, each paying one shilling for a two-course hot meal and one penny for a cup of tea. Meals were served daily Monday to Saturday from noon to 2 p.m. The kitchen was well-equipped with steam ovens and boilers as well as dishwashers and an electric potato peeler. The restaurant had a capacity of 1,000 meals a day; 13,301 meals were served within the first two months, and by May 1943, the restaurant was self -supporting. In November 1944, the restaurant opened for teas on Friday and Saturday afternoons from 3.30 p.m. to 5.30 p.m.; high tea cost one shilling, and plain tea cost eight pence. The restaurant closed on 8 February 1947.

A Film Star's Visit

At the beginning of May, Robert Newton 'the famous film star' was in the audience at the Odeon cinema watching his film *Hatter's Castle* in which he played one of the leading roles as James Brodie. Robert Newton would go on to immortalise the role of Long John Silver in the 1950 Disney film *Treasure Island*, which was mostly shot on location in England and at Denham Studios in Buckinghamshire.

The Czechoslovak Army Band

One of the 'exile' military formations in the country was the Czechoslovak Army-in-exile and several units were stationed in the area for varying periods. The Czechoslovak Army Band and Camp Band proved very popular and a June concert in the Odeon Cinema raised £130 divided between Yeovil hospital and Yeovil nursing association.

Yeovil's Women's Hostel

During the summer, the Young Women's Christian Association (YWCA) opened a women's hostel over Lloyds Bank on the Borough for members of the women's forces. The difficulty in acquiring suitable premises had held up the provision of the much need hostel for many months but now that it had opened the *Yeovil Review* commented in June that 'There can be little doubt our uniformed lady friends of the three Services will take full advantage of the privileges and facilities offered and where a welcome awaits them.' The hostel closed in August 1947.

7

1943

Some Important Events

14 January	Casablanca Conference demands German unconditional surrender.
2 February	German 6th Army surrenders at Stalingrad.
12 May	German and Axis Forces surrender in North Africa.
Night of 16–17 May	RAF 617 Squadron attacks the Ruhr dams—The 'Dam Busters'.
10 July	Allied landings on Sicily.
25 July	Mussolini's Fascist Italian Government overthrown.
3 September	Allied landings at Salerno.
3 September	Italy signs an armistice and German forces occupy the part of Italy not in Allied hands.

Waste Not

At the outbreak of the war, the government knew that the salvaging of essential materials would play an important part in the war effort. Scrap iron, aluminium, metal utensils, glass, rubber, rags, bones, paper, and many other types of recyclable material were collected in cities, towns, and villages. At the end of 1940, government regulations were introduced to make the salvaging and recovery of all such essentials compulsory.

In March 1943, the borough council reported that during the preceding two months, 106 tons of metal, 5 tons of rubber, 2 tons of bones, and just over 1 ton of rags had been collected in the town by the end of March. The collection of wastepaper was also a major item of salvage, and during 1942, over 433,400 tons had been collected nationwide. By the end of 1942, it was estimated that 60 per cent of all paper manufactured in the country came from recycled paper products. Books were collected, but in addition to being used for paper production, many of those in good condition were used to restock libraries destroyed by enemy bombing or sent to the armed forces. In Yeovil during the first six months of 1943, the borough council carried out a 'Book Recovery Drive' which resulted in over 90,000 books being collected and distributed: 8,520 to HM Forces; 1,800 to restocking bombed libraries; and to the Ministry of Supply for pulping, 79,000.

During summer 1941, the borough council began collecting kitchen waste for pig food, collection bins were placed in every residential street and emptied several times a week, white bands were painted around each bin as a precaution against pedestrians colliding with it in the blackout. A depot was set up for receiving and steaming the waste food, which was then sold to local pig farmers initially for £2 per ton. The council estimated that the scheme would result in keeping some 450 pigs and the annual production of 900 sides of bacon. During May and June 1943, just over 124 tons of kitchen waste was collected and sold for £248. With pig bins on every street, there were problems—bins were tipped over by hooligans, scraps were stolen by householders to feed their poultry, and non-edible items were left, such as knives, forks, and spoons. Pig bins remained part of street 'furniture' for some years after the war, and with the availability of explosive fireworks (bangers), blowing off the bin lids was a regular feature during the run-up to the 5 November bonfire night

Ornamental iron railings and gates were a prominent feature of the front gardens of Yeovil residential areas built in the thirty or so years before 1914. Today, apart from iron stubs, few (if any) of the original railings and gates remain.

Towards the end of 1941, the Ministry of Supply ordered local authorities to carry out a survey of iron railings and gates in their areas with the view to their removal to provide scrap iron for the war effort. Only railings and gates required for safety reasons, to enclose cattle or which had special artistic or historic merit, could be excluded.

An article in the *Yeovil Review* of August 1942 explained how the railings and other iron material would help towards providing tanks and guns. A moderate-sized garden gate would supply the metal parts to make five Bren guns, and 2 Cwt of iron railings was equivalent in weight to two radiators for tanks.

In November 1942, the borough council was informed that the removal of all railings and gates had been completed, including those around St John's churchyard, Sidney Gardens, and Bides Garden, and the quantity of metal recovered amounted to 348 tons.

However, the indiscriminate removal of all railings meant that much of the iron was not suitable for munitions manufacture and it seems that much of the scrap was quietly disposed of.

Wings for Victory Week

'Wings for Victory Week' was a countrywide fundraising event organised by national savings in 1943 to help finance the construction of aircraft for the RAF and the Fleet Air Arm. Local savings groups were free to decide the date, and in Yeovil and district, this would be the week beginning Saturday the 8th to Saturday 15 May. The target was £425,000—sufficient to build eighty-five Seafires, the naval version of the Spitfire. At the time, Seafires were being built in the Westland Works, and over 1,670 were constructed by the firm during the war.

Wings for Victory Week was formally opened by Air Chief Marshal, Sir Philip Joubert, KBC, CMG, DSO, inspector-general of the RAF, who took the salute at a march-past through the Borough by contingents from the RAF, the Royal Navy, the army and local civil defence units led by the band of RAF Flying Training Command. Overhead, there was an aerial salute and aerobatics which according to the *Western Gazette* 'delighted the crowd but made the speech making difficult'.

An indicator board showing the amounts collected each day had been erected on the vacant bomb site in the Borough, and following the opening ceremony, a fireman climbed up a ladder and fixed figures showing that on the first day £71,000 had been collected.

The week would be crowded with daily attractions and events designed by the organisers to have the widest appeal. These would include concerts, dances, athletic sports, cricket, boxing, whist drives, a shop window competition, and the youth day and parade would end the week.

Two of the most popular attractions that drew the crowds were the Link Trainer, an early flight simulator for training aircrews, set up in

Messrs Douglas Seaton's Clarence Street motor showrooms, and the Seafire and Spitfire parts exhibition, together with daily parachute packing demonstrations by the Women's Royal Naval Service (WRNS or the 'WRENS') in Messrs Vincent's Princes Street car showrooms.

A large bomb (real but of course containing no explosive) was placed by the indicator board in the Borough, and people were asked to stick savings stamps on it. None of them, it seems, were stolen.

A 'Mystery Man', namely Mr Greer of Beaconfield Road, was at large in the town centre on Saturday afternoon and was finally run to earth in the Market Street veterinary practice by Miss Hodges of 232 Goldcroft, who claimed the prize of savings certificates. However, Tuesday's 'Mystery Lady', Mrs Greer, was not unmasked.

Two Saturday evening dances opened the week's entertainments, the Wessex Electricity Company's was in the Grass Royal school hall and the ARP social sections in the hall at Summerleaze Park.

On Sunday 9 May, a concert was given in the Gaumont cinema by the RAF Flying Training Command Band and up at the Mudford Road playing fields, the cricket match between Yeovil police and a Mr Fox's XI resulted in a win for the 'Fox men' by 111 runs to thirty-three.

During Monday evening, members of the Air Training Corps (ATC) and the Girls' Training Corps combined at Summerleaze Park school to entertain with a programme of gymnastics, songs, and instrumental pieces; meanwhile, in the Park School hall, the Yeovil 1st Company, The Boys' Brigade, presented the concert 'Good Gang'. The national fire service cabaret and dance in the Assembly Rooms was enjoyed by some 300 dancers on Monday evening.

Yeovil Rotary club sponsored a concert by personnel from HMS *Heron* at Grass Royal school on Tuesday evening, and in the Assembly Rooms, girls from the Charles Edward Brooks school, evacuated to Yeovil from London, entertained an audience of over 200, to an evening of song and dance.

Mr York's Juvenile Orchestra gave a concert at Grass Royal school during the following evening. At the Huish football ground, the armed forces women's services, civil defence, police, and the women's land army were among the competitors in an inter-service athletic sports, but the *Western Gazette* reported that 'There was a rather disappointingly small crowd'.

Thursday saw the matron and staff of Yeovil hospital organising a trail of pennies along Kingston and Princes Street. The nurses wore sashes with the printed slogan 'Pennies for Seafires to Help to Win the War'. Some 350 townsfolk attended the Mayor's Ball in the Assembly Rooms that evening; over £100 was raised at the event.

Friday was Farmers' Day, and at the town's weekly produce and cattle markets, collections were made among the farmers and locals; at Messrs R. B. Taylor's market, the auction of a dozen (very scarce) lemons raised the not inconsiderable sum (by 1943's values) of £7 17s 6d. The home guard's Borough company's dance at the Southville drill hall brought in another £40.

On Friday evening at the Huish ground, there was a boxing tournament including two international bouts between the United States and the British army and six British inter-service contests. The international ended honours even, the US won the heavyweight and the British the light-heavyweight contests. In the inter-service bouts, the Commandos, Royal Artillery, and Fleet Air Arm all scored wins. Two sailors entertained the crowd with 'blind boxing and some amusing antics'.

Wings for Victory Week concluded on Saturday afternoon with the Youth Day and Parade. Several hundred young people, including members of the Boys' and Girls' Brigades, ATC, Army Cadet Force, Girls' Training Corps. and local secondary schools, assembled on the town station forecourt, and led by the bands of The Boys' Brigade and the ATC, marched through the crowd-lined streets to Sidney Gardens. Here, they formed three sides of a square facing the bandstand (burnt down in 1972) to be addressed by Captain M. Thomas, DSO, RN, on the useful work which could be done by young people to aid the war effort; following this, they marched to the Huish football ground for an afternoon of athletic sports.

The final social event was the Sunday afternoon concert in the Odeon Cinema 'Fleet Air Arm Fanfare', which was opened by Lt-Cdr D. Lewin DSO, DSC, RN, who addressed the audience on the importance of air cover for the Navy and which the purchase of the eighty-five Seafires would help to maintain. The concert included music in 'the Modern style' and 'Stringbag Jive' dedicated to the 'Fleet Air Arm Veteran, the Swordfish'.

'Wings for Victory Week' proved to have been successful beyond the organisers' expectations; a total of £476,661 was raised enough to buy ninety-five Seafires.

Holidays at Home Week, 1943

Travel during the Second World War could be long, tedious, and very difficult. Petrol for private use was tightly controlled and non-existent for recreational motoring; also, the war effort took priority on rail and road. The discomfort of rail travel can be imagined when a check at Waterloo station during the August bank holiday weekend in 1943 revealed that over 1,300 people had travelled in a main line train, which normally carried 460.

'Holidays at Home' was the national scheme to provide entertainment for the many people who could not (or did not) wish to get away during the usual summer holiday weeks. The Yeovil holidays amenities committee worked hard to organise a varied programme of entertainment and designated the week (which ran from Saturday 31 July to Sunday 8 August) as 'Holiday at Home Week 1943'.

On Saturday 31 July, between 700 and 800 people paid their one shilling entrance fee and attended the Great Sports Attraction on the Westland sports ground. The sports included foot races, relay races, cycle races, long and high jumps, and tugs-of-war, with competitors entering from the local civilian population and the army at Houndstone camps; soldiers won the flat mile race and the men's relay, but the Yeovil police team won the tug-of-war. The children enjoyed a Punch and Judy show presented by Corporal Stafford, the well-known 'Uncle Tommy' on west regional radio.

A concert was given in the Assembly Rooms by the Fleet Air Arm Dance Orchestra, who presented 'Band Waggon' in aid of the Merchant Navy Comforts Fund. Guest artistes included BBC pianist Ernest Lush and Johnny Fanton, formerly resident guest artiste with the Columbia Broadcasting Company; Paddy Dolan and 'Chips' Chappell provided the comedy routines.

A full programme was arranged for bank holiday Monday, 2 August. At 2.30 p.m., Westland Aircraft played Yeovil in a cricket match on the company's sports ground; Westland won by four runs. A monster whist drive was held at Huish junior school at 7.30 p.m., and there were dances in Summerleaze Park school hall, music by Billy Kelly and Orchestra, and at the Assembly Rooms with the Divisional Dance Orchestra directed by Mons. Paquay.

However, the highlight of the day—a Speedway meeting on Mr Chudleigh's field at the Pen Mills, which included a Ladies' pillion event and a chance for an enthusiast—was cancelled at the last moment due to the non-arrival by rail of the racing fuel. During the day, Mr Schofield, the organiser, had toured the local railway stations trying to find out what had happened to the precious petrol and had tried unsuccessfully to obtain supplies from local petrol dealers.

On Tuesday, 3 August, Grass Royal school hall was filled to capacity, with many people standing, for a two-hour entertainment presented by the Westland Players and an ENSA party. The Westland Players performed a farcical comedy 'Brown with an E', which was reported to have 'harmonised well with the holiday mood of the audience'. ENSA presented instrumental music, songs and dances described as being 'both "hot" and "sweet"'. Lena Fordyce danced and Shenton Harris sang.

On Wednesday afternoon, a large crowd turned out at the Huish football ground to watch an exhibition baseball game by two visiting teams of American servicemen. In the evening, the Americans drew another large audience to the Assembly Rooms for a concert of Spirituals and Gospel songs followed by a 'jam session' from The Rhythm Boys.

Over 1,000 people attended a horse and pony gymkhana at the Huish football ground on Thursday afternoon. Despite the entries being limited to horses and ponies kept within 15 miles of Yeovil because of transport difficulties, the twelve events attracted 182 entries. No professional riders took part, but the standard of jumping was reported to have been very good on the slippery course; the young riders were said to have done well in the conditions. The Sherborne Boys' Brigade band played selections during the afternoon. On Thursday evening, an 'Under Twenty's Dance' organised by Yeovil junior youth council (with Mr Jack Willey as MC) was held at Grass Royal school, and Ron Webb's Savoy Orchestra played at the 'Popular Dance' in the Assembly Rooms; admission was three shillings, with Forces paying two shillings, all proceeds to the Red Cross Prisoners of War Parcels Fund.

There was a whist Drive in Reckleford school on Friday evening— a quiet day.

On Saturday afternoon, 7 August, 'A Great Children's Fancy Dress Parade and Competition' assembled in Sidney Gardens at 1.30 p.m., and at 2 p.m., the eighty entrants marched behind the band of the 1st Yeovil Company of the Boys' Brigade to the Huish ground. The prize winners were 'A Lord Mayor', 'Schoolmaster', 'Modern Girl', 'Eighth Army', 'A Squander Bug', 'Save for Victory', 'John Bull', 'Wooden Soldier', 'Salvage' and the two 'Prettiest Children' prize winners were 'Gypsy Girl' and 'Puck'. The parade was followed by school children's sports with some 280 entries.

The Yeovil and district horticultural society, the town allotments association, Somerset beekeepers' association, and Yeovil cage birds society held an open show of vegetables, fruit, flowers, honey, and cage birds on Saturday afternoon in the South Street Baptist Sunday school rooms, with 422 entries. Several hundred people visited the show, which raised £110 for the Red Cross Prisoners of War Parcels Fund.

The last dance of the Holidays at Home Week 1943 was held in the Assembly Rooms with Billy Kelly and his Orchestra providing the music.

The final event of the week was a united service and *carolare* on Sunday evening in Sidney Gardens, where a section of the Yeovil Philharmonic Society accompanied the hymn singing.

Around the Town in 1943

Wardens 'Under Fire'

A 'Wardens' service instruction and quiz' was held in the Park School hall on the evening of Saturday 20 March among the town's five warden sectors. The evening embraced all forms of wardens' duties; the quiz questions ranged from how to approach and effect a rescue from a crashed aircraft, the ways and means of destroying mustard gas, to what to do in the event of invasion. The final result was first, north; second, west; third, south; fourth, Preston; and fifth, east.

A False Alarm

On the evening of Wednesday 24 March, the Yeovil national fire service received a telephone call to a fire in Court Ash. On arrival, this turned out to be a false alarm, and it was reported that two boys were seen leaving the telephone kiosk in Court Ash near the Odeon cinema.

Changes at the Liberal Club

In April 1943, the Liberal Club's general committee agreed to appoint a billiards room steward to relieve the bar steward of this duty. The post was advertised at a weekly wage of £3 10s, the hours to be 9 a.m.–noon, 2–5 p.m., and 6.30–10.30 p.m. for seven days, with one half-day off and one hour taken for tea. Of the four applicants, Mr P. Winsor of 6 Park Street was appointed, commencing on Monday 17 May. The committee also decided that the bar and new billiards stewards could partake in games, providing it did not interfere with their duties. However, Mr Winsor gave up on health grounds after only a week, and Mr W. F. Allen was appointed after a ballot by ten votes to three over his rival, Mr H. Templeman. Mr Allen resigned on health grounds in December 1943 and Mr G. Hawkins was appointed new billiards steward.

It was decided to place a notice in the bar stating 'No Betting Transactions are Allowed on Club Premises'. Mr Deacon was appointed to represent the club on the borough council's committee for entertaining the American forces.

Lemons

Mr W. R. Hopkins, serving with the RAF in North Africa, sent home eight lemons (a little-seen luxury); these were auctioned in aid of the British Red Cross Prisoners of War Fund. Four auctioned by Mrs Hopkins raised £5 14s and the remaining four, auctioned at Westland's offices, realised £3 1s 6d. Crew 'E' of Yeovil centre of the observer corps raised £65 for the prisoners of war fund through a whist drive, various stalls, and a tea with entertainment given by the Yeovil literary and dramatic society, in a marquee in Mr West's garden at 83 West Coker.

Enterprising Youngsters

Wanting to do their bit for the Wings Appeal fund, the June *Yeovil Review* reported that the following young people had carried out some fundraising of their own:

Sheila and Michael Quinn, 91 Hillcrest Road, exhibition of rabbits, 15s
Pat Morgan, 126 West Coker Road, sale of lemon, £1
Jean Hawker, 12 Matthews Road, raffle, 15s
Hazel Andrews, Huish, gift to national savings, 2s 6d
Jean Lucas, 27 Sparrow Road, sale of kettle holders, 7s 6d
Anthony Bond, exhibition of posters, Preston district, £1 6s 1d
Jean Pollard, Free Gift, 10s

In the Borough Juvenile Court

In July 1943, two brothers, aged eight and nine, appeared before the Borough juvenile court charged with stealing precision band instruments (drum and drumsticks and two pairs of cymbals) from St Andrew's school, Preston Grove, during the Whitsun holidays.

The *Western Gazette* reported that the prosecution was brought by Yeovil education committee represented by Mr A. R. McMillan, the deputy town clerk, who said that the committee was sorry to bring two such young boys before the court, but it was hoped the action would be a warning and deterrent to other boys and girls. In a statement to the police, the younger boy stated his brother had intended to sell the instruments and buy a box for some rabbits. Their mother had told them to take the things back. Alderman W. J. C. Pittard, the chairman, stated that it was the parent's duty to take responsibility and prevent children from doing wrong. He believed that a mother's insistence on taking the instruments back had had far more influence on the boys than bringing them to court. The case was dismissed.

The responsibility of parents was emphasised in another case, when three brothers aged fifteen, thirteen, and twelve years old, were charged with committing fifteen shillings worth of damage to Mr Arthur Powell's hayrick in a field near Ninesprings. The justices dismissed the case on payment of costs of shillings with the suggestion to the boys' father that the money be kept out of their pocket money. Inspector Dredge said the police received numerous complaints of such damage, which appeared to be due to lack of parental control. The chairman told the boys, 'It is not fun to do anything that is going to hurt other people', and told the father that the boys' behaviour depended on the influence of the parents, who had a duty to keep their children in check.

Closed for Holiday and Tell Your Warden
Messrs Neal and Williams' hardware shop on Middle Street closed from Saturday morning, 31 July to Friday morning, 6 August, for the staff annual holiday.

Ladies' hairdressers Swanson's closed their salons on South Street and Hendford for their two weeks' holiday on Monday 9 August.

Residents were asked to tell their air raid warden before they left on holiday where they would be staying and where the keys for their houses, etc., could be obtained in case of emergency such as an air raid.

The ATS Band
The thirty-six female members band of the Auxiliary Territorial Service (ATS) under their conductor, Sgt Morris of the Welsh Regiment, gave a concert of 'popular' music in the Borough on Tuesday evening, 27 July.

A New Headmaster
The new headmaster of Yeovil School following the retirement of the Reverend J. W. Pearson, MA, was Mr Arthur Denys Halstead Thompson,

MA (Hons), who had been released from his position as temporary assistant at the air ministry. His previous teaching posts had been assistant master at Hitchin Grammar school, and senior English master at Gresham's School, Holt in Norfolk.

Mr Thompson would retire from Yeovil School in 1962 and was the author of a well-known and widely used series of English books.

8

1944

Some Important Events

22 January	Allied landings at Anzio.
27 January	Siege of Leningrad (St Petersburg) ends after nearly two and a half years.
May	Over 1,500,000 US Army personnel in Great Britain preparing for D-Day.
4 June	Allies capture Rome.
6 June	D-Day landings in Normandy begin the liberation of Nazi-occupied Western Europe.
20 July	Failed assassination of Adolf Hitler.
15 August	Allied landings in the South of France
25 August	Paris liberated.
3 September	Brussels and Antwerp liberated.
17–26 September	Battle of Arnhem.
4 November	Greece liberated.
16 December	German Army attack in the Ardennes—Battle of the Bulge.

For Valour

The name of Lieutenant Alec George Horwood, VC, DCM, The Queen's Royal Regiment (West Surrey), was added to the Yeovil Borough war memorial at a ceremony attended by his only daughter, family, and friends in July 2012.

Londoner Alec Horwood, as a sergeant in The Queen's Royal Regiment (West Surrey), had been captured while attending a wounded comrade during the Dunkirk evacuation in 1940 but had escaped via Antwerp; for his gallant action, he was awarded the Distinguished Conduct Medal (DCM). In April 1941, while stationed at Houndstone camp, he met and married Madeline Dove, whose parents lived at Wraxhill Road and had one daughter.

Following the grant of a commission, Lt Horwood was serving in the Burma campaign and was attached to the 1st Battalion, Northampton Regiment, in heavy fighting on 18, 19, and 20 January 1944. It was during this time that his outstanding bravery was recognised by the award of the Victoria Cross.

The citation in the *London Gazette* on 30 March 1944 reads as follows:

At Kyauchaw on 18th January 1944, Lieutenant Horwood accompanied the forward company of The Northamptonshire Regiment into action against a Japanese defended locality with his forward mortar observation post. Throughout that day he lay in an exposed position which had been completely bared of cover by concentrated air bombing and effectively shot his own mortars and those of a half troop of another unit while the company was manoeuvring to locate the exact position of the enemy bunkers and machine-gun nests. During the whole of this time Lieutenant Horwood was under intense sniper, machine-gun and mortar fire, and at night came back with most valuable information about the enemy.

On 19th January, he moved forward with another company and established an observation post on a precipitous ridge. From here, while under continual fire from the enemy, he directed accurate mortar fire in support of two attacks which were put in during the day. He also carried out a personal reconnaissance along and about the bare ridge, deliberately drawing the enemy fire so that the fresh company which he led to the position, and which was to carry out an attack, might see the enemy positions.

Lieutenant Horwood remained on the ridge during the night 19th–20th January and on the morning of the 20th January shot the mortars again to support a fresh attack by another company put in from the rear of the enemy. He was convinced that the enemy would crack and volunteered to lead the attack planned for that afternoon. He led this attack with such calm resolute bravery, that the enemy were reached and while standing up in the wire, directing and leading the men with complete disregard to the enemy fire which was then at point blank range, he was mortally wounded.

By his fine example of leadership on the 18th, 19th and 20th January when continually under fire, by his personal example to others of reconnoitring, guiding and bringing up ammunition in addition to his duties at the mortar observation post, all of which were carried out under great physical difficulties and in exposed positions, this officer set the highest example of bravery and devotion to duty which all ranks responded to magnificently. The cool, calculated actions of this officer, coupled with his magnificent bearing and bravery which culminated in his death on the enemy wire, very largely contributed to the ultimate success of the operation which resulted in the capture of the enemy position.

Salute the Soldier Week, 1944

Saturday 6 May to Saturday 13 May 1944 was 'Salute the Soldier Week', the national savings campaign for 1944, and the Yeovil and district's savings target was £425,000 invested in bonds, savings certificates, stamps, etc., and sufficient to equip a battalion of the Somerset Light Infantry for a year. Clubs, streets, individuals, and firms large and small entered the spirit of the week, setting themselves savings targets. Westland Aircraft's target of £30,000 with the slogan 'Change your pay for battle array' reached £36,679.

Events during the week included parades, dances, concerts, sports, and the ceremony in King George Street when each day's savings total was marked up on an indicator above the main entrance to Frederick Taylor's department store. The indicator represented a gun firing at a target, and the trajectory of the shell showed the daily sum invested in national savings.

On Saturday afternoon 6 May, with flags flying to the music of the Band of the King's Dragoon Guards, a procession of units of all the fighting forces, women's services, pre-service training corps, civil defence, voluntary aid detachments, Red Cross, the US army, and local home guard units marched from Wyndham Fields through the Borough, where General Sir George Jeffreys, MP, took the salute, and on to the Huish football ground for the official opening ceremony. At the ground, hundreds of townspeople gathered for the ceremony to be carried out by the general, who was accompanied by the mayor, Alderman W. S. Vosper, Sir George Davies, Member of Parliament for the Yeovil Division, Lady Davies, and Mrs Horwood, the widow of Lt A. G. Horwood VC, DCM.

General Jeffreys addressed the audience and stated that as a former commander of the Wessex Division from 1926 to 1930, which had included a Somerset territorial battalion, he believed the people of Yeovil were proud of the past history and present performance of their splendid county regiment, and he hoped and prayed that after the war, the following lines written over 300 years ago would no longer apply: 'God and the soldier we alike adore, when at the brink of ruin, but not before. After deliverance and the wrong requited, God is forgotten and the soldier slighted.' The general went on to say that 'We should forget neither God nor the soldier but set our house in order, trust the Lord and keep our powder dry!'

The week that followed carried a full programme of entertainments and sporting events. On the opening Saturday afternoon, a 'portrait gallery' of about 1,000 photographs of local servicemen and women was opened in the Park School hall and an exhibition of military equipment was held in Douglas Seaton's car showrooms.

There were several football competitions on the Mudford Road playing fields, an athletics meeting, and a horse and pony gymkhana on the Huish football ground. The American soldiers from Houndstone camp entered into the spirit of the week with a baseball match on the Mudford Road playing fields and an American invitation ball in the Assembly Rooms with some 350 guests dancing to 'A GI Dance Band'.

A highlight of the week was the 'Stars' open-air 'all-in' wrestling and boxing tournament before an audience of over 2,000 people at the Huish ground on Friday 12 May. The *Western Gazette* reported:

> An outstanding attraction was the 'all-in' wrestling match between the world champion (cruiserweight) Sgt Jimmy Britt, US Army and Private Cecil ('Rough House') Wilkins of the Canadian army, British Empire champion (cruiserweight). The silver cup was presented to Britt by Colonel L.W. Brown, US Army.
>
> The boxing 'high spot' of the evening was the exhibition contest between Sgt Freddy Mills. RAF, British Empire heavy-weight boxing champion, and his sparring partner Sgt Joe Carter, RAF.

Entertainments included dances at Grass Royal school and a Westland-sponsored ball in the Assembly Rooms, which was also the venue for the home guard dance. Concerts were arranged by various organisations and firms. The national fire service presented a full programme of music in the Odeon cinema, with the guest appearance of Ralph Reader of 'Film and Radio Gang Show fame' and a concert in aid of the Red Cross prisoners war parcels fundraised £105. The York Variety Orchestra gave a concert before a full house in Grass Royal school, and the Americans presented a 'musical comedy premiere' in Summerleaze Park school.

Westland's Salute the Soldier committee presented '"Seaside Revels" by our Weymouth Girls' and Marco Lavonte, the magician, assisted by Dolores. The War Workers' Club gave a variety show at Grass Royal school, and Mr W. S. Rendell arranged the showing of films of commando raids in Norway and the army's campaign in North Africa plus a supporting programme in Mr Norman's garage off West Coker Road. The shift workers organised an ankle and leg competition, which attracted over forty ladies to enter the ankle competition, but an undisclosed number of men entered the best-shaped gentleman's leg and the most comical.

The *Western Gazette* reported the baby show in the Park School hall on 11 May:

> [It] provided a traffic problem when Yeovil's bonniest babes—at least 111 of them, with their mothers, grandmothers, friends and perambulators converged on the Hall, and Mr. Redwood opened up his garden as a garage for perambulators to ease the traffic problem.

Yeovil and district's Salute the Soldier Week raised just over £460,000 and within a month the allies would be storming ashore on the Normandy beaches. Battalions of the Somerset Light Infantry would fight through to VE-Day in May 1945 with the famous 43rd Wessex Division.

D-Day, 6 June 1944

On 6 June 1944, the Allies stormed ashore on the Normandy coast, and with the Russian armies pressing in from the east, the fate of Nazi Germany was sealed. Although all eyes and thoughts were on the strip of coast across the English Channel, here is a quick look back to what was happening here in Yeovil during that momentous first week of June.

The war was affecting everyday life, and a Yeovil grocer was brought before the borough magistrates for supplying soap to the proprietor of a cafe without the necessary ration documents. To be sent to prison, he told the bench, would be a holiday from his business worries, and he pointed out that there were over 7,500 rules about rationed goods laid down by the Ministry of Food. The grocer explained that he did his best to comply, but counting thousands of ration coupons and making returns, in addition to routine work with depleted staff, meant that there could be unintentional oversights. He had been labouring for a long time under considerable difficulties; he had lost his staff of three men; his wife had been ill for eighteen months; and he was left with only a young girl as an assistant to deal with the issue of 4,000 rations. The grocer and the proprietor of the cafe, however, were fined £1 each for the offence.

The magistrates also dealt with nine cases of keeping dogs without a licence; all were found guilty and fined 10 shillings each. Two female cyclists were fined for riding without lights, and a resident of West Coker Road was fined 10 shillings for showing the light from a reading lamp during the blackout despite the claim that it had been switched on by a three-year-old child. However, two summonses against a local publican for failing to sign the register for attending as a fireguard and performing his statutory fire-watching duties were withdrawn.

The bench was asked to approve the opening of the town's cinemas at 2.30 p.m. on Sundays, instead of 6.30 p.m., as the servicemen visiting the town had nothing to do on those afternoons. The secretary of the executive for entertainment for the services, who presented the application, stated that there was no question of keeping the men out of the churches or places of worship, but of helping their morale. Despite objections from the local clergy, the magistrates granted the application, but they prohibited the admission of young people under the age of sixteen until 5 p.m. to 'give them the opportunity of going to Sunday School'. During the week of the D-Day landings, the Central cinema was presenting Irving Berlin's *This is the Army* in glorious technicolour with the Original US Army Stars and George Murphy, Joan Leslie, Ronald Reagan, and Irving Berlin singing 'My British Buddy'. At the Odeon, Robert Donat and Greer Garson were appearing in *Good-bye Mr Chips* followed by *Nelson's Touch* with Randolph Scott. Rosalind Russell was starring in *The Beautiful Cheat* at the Gaumont.

On the afternoon of Sunday 4 June, at St Andrew's church, on Preston Grove, a bishop's chair made of oak and carved by Raymond Brothers of Manor Road was dedicated by the vicar of Yeovil, the Rev. E. Mortlock Treen. The chair bore the inscription 'Given for the service of God and in grateful remembrance of Maud Josephine Paynter by the teachers, old scholars and children of St Andrew's Sunday school'. For many years, Mrs Paynter was the Sunday school superintendent.

With so many men in the armed forces and the great need for war production, there was plenty of work for women, with advertisements for all sorts of jobs; one called to women of the district to take part in the war effort and 'Work on Aircraft Locally'. They were asked 'Can YOU come Full Time? If not, come Part Time' for the many interesting and worthwhile jobs.

However, life was not all work, and if you felt like a night out, there was the home guard dance at East Coker hall to Harry Virgin and His Band on Friday 9 June; no doubt, there was a lot to talk about that evening.

On D-Day, the author was seven years and two months old and has one memory of one of the days that changed the world: watching aircraft flying overhead and hearing his father saying that they were on their way to the invasion. Clearer, however, are the memories of the time when the Americans were in and around Yeovil during the build-up of forces for the invasion. The streets were packed with military vehicles of all descriptions, there were American GIs everywhere and he recalled cycling with his father along Thorne Lane (it was truly a lane then) passing halftracks, lorries, and jeeps.

One memory that does stand out is the morning he was on his way through Huish to school in South Street, when columns of GIs in full combat gear came marching along; although he could not know at the time, they were on their way to entrain at Pen Mill station bound for Weymouth and the invasion fleet. As the soldiers passed, they handed out candy and packets of the treasured chewing gum as we stood and watched them on their way to war; he has often wondered how many survived.

Possibly some of those hundreds of GIs who marched through Huish on that June morning in 1944 came back to Yeovil because the Americans had established two general hospitals at Lufton and Houndstone camps.

The Second Evacuation

Just over a week after the D-Day landings on 6 June, the first V-1 flying bomb (Doodlebug) landed and exploded in Hackney, London, killing six people. So began the German attacks by the V-1s, followed in November by the V-2 rockets.

As the attacks on London and the Home Counties grew in intensity during June and into July, thousands of children were evacuated away from the area and many came to Yeovil from Surrey. The youngsters arrived on special trains at Yeovil Junction during Monday and Tuesday 10 and 11 July; some 500 were billeted with families in Yeovil and in the villages around the town.

On arrival, the children were given a hot meal at the British restaurant in the Liberal club and then transported to Summerleaze Park school and St Gilda's convent, in The Avenue. Here, they were medically examined and then taken to the homes where they would stay until it was deemed safe for the youngsters to return.

The leaders of the party told the *Western Gazette* that they were very much impressed by the helpful way in which the children had been received into Yeovil and district homes and expressed their sincere thanks to all the people of the area for their hospitality. The *Gazette* further reported that the response to the loudspeaker vans that had toured the town on the Sunday prior to the evacuees' arrival asking for accommodation in local homes had been such that the borough council did not have to use its compulsory billeting powers.

The majority of the youngsters left for home by a special train from Yeovil Junction on Wednesday 6 December, with 240 coming from Yeovil and over 200 from the villages. On 13 December, the *Western Gazette* wrote:

> The Mayor (Mr. W.S. Vosper) was at the station to 'say goodbye' and he told them how much Yeovil had enjoyed having them. Miss Osborne (Chairman of the Rural Evacuation Committee) also spoke. The masters and mistresses and escorts accompanying the children returned thanks and the children cheered the Mayor and his supporters. Miss Osborne reported to the Rural Council on Friday, that most of the children were terribly disappointed they could not stay for Christmas.

Sixty years later, on 12 July 2004, two of the evacuees—Mr Peter Durrant and Mrs Sheila Nicholas—returned to Yeovil and were welcomed at Yeovil Junction by the mayor, Councillor Ian Martin. The pair were then driven around the town, and although they found some parts were still familiar, much of Yeovil was now unrecognisable. Mr Durrant had stayed with coal merchant's widow, Mrs Durrant, in Vincent Street, the street now buried under the bus station. Mrs Nicholas had lodged with Mr and Mrs Bright at Westbourne Grove and found the road and surrounding area very much the same as she remembered it.

Following the town tour, the former evacuees were entertained in the mayor's parlour before they returned home.

In August 1944

A Yeovil resident in Park Street was brought before the town magistrates on 1 August charged with allowing 'an unscreened light to show after black-out'. Police war reservist Roberts told the bench that on seeing the light in an upstairs bedroom he had knocked on the offender's front door but had received no reply. However, a neighbour appeared and informed the officer that the resident was deaf. Reservist Roberts stated that he had obtained a ladder, climbed up, and (finding the window slightly ajar) opened it; reaching in, he shook 'the gentleman awake'. Despite some amusement in the court, the offender was fined 10 shillings—a hefty fine at the time.

Yeovil's firefighters of the national fire service had a busy six days in August 1944. In the early hours of Thursday the 10th, fire broke out in a sitting room on the second floor of the Manor hotel. The sound of the blaze woke the manageress who dressed quickly and ran the few hundred yards from Hendford to the fire station in South Street to raise the alarm. Led by column officer C. O. Mitchell, several fire crews were on site within minutes and found the room blazing fiercely and flames roaring over 20 feet from the window.

While the blaze was confined to the sitting room, the staff were successfully evacuated from their quarters on the top floor. Apart from one of the waitresses who had tried to go back to her room and had to be rescued overcome by smoke, no one was hurt. The fire was brought under control within half an hour, but it took another two hours to put it out. The sitting room was completely gutted, an adjoining office was badly damaged, and there was considerable smoke and water damage to other parts of the hotel. The cause of the blaze could not be found.

That afternoon, the Yeovil firemen were called to Manor Farm, at Rimpton, where four large ricks of hay, straw, and corn were ablaze and endangering outbuildings on an adjoining small-holding. Once again, column officer Mitchell commanded the operation, which lasted over forty hours and involved relief crews working in shifts.

A third fire during the same afternoon broke out in a wooden cricket pavilion in Preston Plucknett, but the crew sent to the blaze arrived too late to save the building, which was completely destroyed. No cause could be found, but the fire was considered suspicious.

The crew called to a suspected chimney fire at 37 Coronation Avenue on the following Monday (14 August) found that the smoke was coming through a crack in the cavity wall from the neighbour's faulty boiler flue.

Wednesday the 16th was another busy day for the Yeovil men, when a crew was called out in the morning to reinforce teams tackling a large rick fire at Greinton, near Street, Somerset. Two hours later, a call was received from Sparkford Saw Mills that a fire had broken out in a sawn timber stack, and it was burning fiercely when the two fire engines arrived on the scene. The blaze took over three hours to bring under control and extinguish.

Finally, the editor of the *Western Gazette* received the following letter from Mr John English, the district secretary of the Transport and General Workers' Union, and published it on 4 August:

Sir,—We are constantly having letters at this office from members of the Union, asking us to do something for workers who are often left stranded after a long day's work, due to the crowding out of 'buses by shoppers. This is particularly so in the case of Crewkerne and Sherborne bound buses. The worse feature appears to be that a considerable number of passengers are only doing very short journeys, which it is considered may well be done at times other than the peak period. Some of these workers are obliged to leave home at 7 a.m. and do not get home until 7 p.m., and if they miss their 'bus for the reason stated above, it often means their being away from home thirteen or fourteen hours. I would therefore be glad if you will insert this appeal to shoppers to do their shopping between 10 and 12 and 2 and 4, leaving the 'buses free for the workers at the peak period.

The record is silent on whether the appeal was heeded.

Around the Town in 1944

The Army Blood Transfusion Service
The *Western Gazette* reminded readers that blood was urgently required by the armed forces and that on 9 and 23 May, the Army Blood

Transfusion Service would be visiting the town. The *Gazette* pointed out that one casualty in every ten could be saved by a blood transfusion and in no other way.

Sunday Morning Service for the US Army

South Street Baptist Church held a morning service on Sunday 30 April for the US Army personnel stationed in the area. The Americans chose the hymns and an US Army chaplin, Captain Hart, gave the address.

Also, the Americans were invited to attend the 'flower service' that evening when the chapel had been decorated with spring flowers by the junior church council under the direction of Mesdames Gardner and Thomas.

Yeovil ARP Skittles League

The results of the ARP skittles league's matches on 3 May:

home guard A: 343—special police A: 322;
Westland ARP: 346—east ward wardens: 323;
north ward wardens: 304—NFS station T: 306;
special police B: 310—home guard B: 320;
ARP headquarters: 354—Preston ward wardens: 368;
Westland home guard: 342—NFS Z: 328

The Sailor's Night Out

The *Western Gazette* of 11 August reported:

A 19 year-old sailor, alleged to have been drunk and disorderly in Reckleford on Wednesday night, told the Yeovil justices on Thursday that 'he did not like the Navy'. Alderman W.J.C. Pittard (chairman): 'You have no right to upset townspeople though you are on leave. This is a fine start in life isn't it?' to which the defendant pointing to his uniform replied 'so is this!'

'Well,' said Alderman Pittard, 'I couldn't choose my job when I was your age.' 'And I can't choose mine either!' defendant retorted.

'That is no excuse,' Alderman Pittard returned. 'That is not my excuse,' replied defendant: 'it was my first shore leave for nine weeks.'

'Even that doesn't merit you getting drunk,' said Alderman Pittard. 'A couple of glasses of beer doesn't do anyone any harm, but it is a different matter when you have to be locked up for the night. You will be fined 7s 6d.'

Damaging a Static Water Tank

In August, an eight-year-old boy, an evacuee from London, was brought up before juvenile court on the prosecution of Mr George Atkinson, Yeovil's chief fire guard officer, charged with putting his thumb through the soft plaster repairs to a static water tank and causing damage amounting to 3s 6d. Mr Atkinson told the court that the case had been brought to warn children and 'others' of the serious complications that could have arisen. In dismissing the case, the justices told the lad that he was banned from going to the cinema for two weeks.

Queues

In wartime Britain, people queued for everything due to wartime rationing and scarcities. Usually, it was not the queuing itself that caused the complaints—the queue was generally accepted; however, it could be other factors that the following letter to the editor of the *Western Gazette* published on 8 August explains:

> 'A Housewife' writes:
>
> Queues in Yeovil
>
> It's no enjoyment to have to stand 1 1/2 hours in biting winds and rain with no shelter whatsoever, but you have to do it, or else walk into an empty shop. Another thing when the goods are delivered why is it you have to wait for an hour or more before the doors are opened? Surely the wives and mothers deserve a little consideration when they have to give up their sons and husbands for the great national effort.

'My America'

Miss Lois Latham from North Carolina and one of the organisers of the American Red Cross Donut Dugout services club in the Newnam Memorial Hall, talked about 'My America' to the Baptist fellowship at South Street Baptist Church on the evening of Monday 9 October. As well as extolling her native home, she expressed her concern with some of the wartime marriages between United States servicemen and British girls. 'Not all the girls realise what they are going out to,' Miss Latham said, 'in States which the depression hit very hard.'

America Calling

On the evening of Wednesday 11 October, Mr Ronald F. Hart, the manager of the Odeon cinema, presented *America Calling* by visiting members of a United States Army concert team. The cinema was packed, and some special guests were American wounded soldiers from the US general hospitals at Houndstone and Lufton. The wounded GIs were served refreshments by the Yeovil Girls' Training Corps.

At the Pictures

Showing in the cinemas during the week commencing Monday 27 November were *Cobra Woman* (in Technicolor) starring Maria Montez, John Hall, and Sabu at the Odeon; *Rebecca* starring Laurence Olivier and Joan Fontaine at the Gaumont; and *In Which We Serve* starring Noel Coward, John Mills, Celia Thompson, and Joyce Carey at the Central.

9

1945: The Year of Victory

Some Important Events

28 January	Battle of the Bulge ends with German defeat.
17 January	Soviet army captures Warsaw.
26 January	Soviet army liberates Auschwitz concentration camp near Krakow.
12 April	President of the United States Franklin D. Roosevelt dies and is succeeded by Harry S. Truman.
13 April	British army liberates Belsen concentration camp.
23 April	Soviet army enters Berlin.
25 April	Mussolini executed by Italian partisans.
30 April	Hitler commits suicide as Soviet army closes in on his Berlin bunker.
2 May	Germany army in Italy surrenders.
2 May	Berlin falls to Soviet army
4 May	German forces in Holland, Denmark, and North-West Germany surrender and on 9 May in Norway.
7 May	Germany surrenders unconditionally.
8 May	Victory in Europe—VE-Day.
9 May	Channel Islands liberated.
5 July	General Election—Conservatives lose to Labour—Prime Minister Winston Churchill is replaced by Clement Atlee.
6 August	Atomic bomb dropped on Hiroshima.
8 August	Soviet Union declares war on Japan.
9 August	Atomic bomb dropped on Nagasaki.
14 August	Japan surrenders.
15 August	Victory over Japan—VJ-Day.

Victory in Europe

At the beginning of May 1945, the announcement of the defeat of Nazi Germany was expected at any time, and across the nation, arrangements were underway to celebrate Victory in Europe—VE-Day—when it arrived. Already, Yeovil had prepared its programme of events, and the pubs had been granted extended opening hours to 11.30 p.m. for the great day.

The author recalls that Monday 7 May was an odd sort of day because everybody seemed to be waiting for something to happen and for Mr Churchill, the prime minister, to tell us that the war was over in Europe, but nothing happened. Then suddenly at 7.40 p.m. in the evening, the BBC announced in a news flash that the Prime Minister would broadcast to the nation at 3 o'clock on the next afternoon, and that Tuesday 8 May would be Victory in Europe Day and a holiday; Wednesday would also be a holiday.

During that Monday evening, cinemagoers at the Odeon were watching Alan Ladd and Lorretta Young in a film with the strangely prophetic title of *And Now Tomorrow*; when the news flash was announced, the audience stood on their seats and cheered.

VE-Day dawned in Yeovil with flags and streamers decorating the town centre, and a good-humoured crowd soon thronged the streets. Many were wearing red, white, and blue ribbons, but they were outdone by an elderly man who strode about wearing a top hat and a frock coat festooned with Union Jacks. All the town's churches and chapels threw open their doors and the noontime services were packed with worshippers. The Boys' and Girls' Brigades, led by their band, marched through the streets following a service in South Street Baptist Church.

At 3 p.m., Winston Churchill announced in his long-awaited broadcast that the hostilities in Europe had officially ceased, and an hour later, the mayor, Councillor William Vosper, standing on a platform built on the 1941 bomb site opposite the present HSBC bank addressed a jubilant crowd in the Borough.

The mayor recounted the events since the war began in September 1939, paying tribute to the nation's fighting forces and our allies during the past five and a half years. In conclusion, he reminded everyone that the war was still going on in the Far East against the Japanese, and he hoped that when the final victory was won, the world could look forward to a long era of peace and prosperity. As the mayor ended his speech, the bells of St John's Church rang out a victory peal, and the people of Yeovil danced in the Borough or marched with arms linked through the town.

The mayor spoke again in the Borough at 7 p.m., calling upon Yeovilians to 'Sing and dance, for this is Victory Day—I want you to enjoy yourselves—well done Yeovil, we can be proud of ourselves!'

The *Western Gazette* recalled that May evening:

The scenes at Yeovil on the night of VE-Day were unequalled on any occasion within memory. The mood of the crowd was one of unrestrained jubilation. Hundreds whirled around in fantastic dances, jitterbugging, laughing, singing and shouting. Music was played by Bill Kelly and his Band and relayed through amplifiers on a National Fire Service van. Scores linked arms and marched vociferously through the streets. When dusk fell the lights in the streets blazed in the Borough, while in Sidney Gardens and Bide's Garden, high powered lamps strung among the trees gave theatrical beauty to the foliage and flower beds. In the centre of the town St. John's grey walls that had withstood bombs in 1941, although some of the windows were damaged, were floodlit. Crowds gathered there, seeking the sense of quietude and peace that were to be found only a stone's throw from the joyous shouts and whirling thousands in the Borough. Tired momentarily with dancing and hoarse from shouting, they lay at ease on the floodlit grass.

A cheer rent the air as the floodlights were turned on, then the revelry was renewed. The noise of fireworks and thunder flashes mingled with the music and the songs. Hour by hour the crowd thickened. The V A.D. Somerset/19 members patrolled the town, and several girls who had danced in rings until they were giddy and fainted were revived—only to begin again.

On and on the band played on and on the dancers danced. Midnight struck. The band had played non-stop since the early evening. They played until they could play no more. The crowd gave them a ringing cheer as they laid down their instruments after the singing of 'Auld Lang Syne' and 'God Save the King'.

The band went home, but the crowd didn't. From nowhere appeared an accordion and hundreds at a time gathered round the single minstrel. Outside the Westminster Bank a large crowd gathered and dancing went on for nearly two hours. Cheering people marched through the streets right up to 3.30 a.m.

It was a night to remember.

At a 10.15 a.m. on 9 May, crowds lined the streets and cheered the mile-long parade of over 1,000 men and women of the three fighting services, civil defence, and the United States Army, as led by three bands; they marched from Sherborne Road to the Huish football ground for the Public Thanksgiving Service. Many thousands of townspeople gathered in and around the ground, and there was cheering and warm applause as the US Army contingent marched in, led by Sgt C. W. Whitaker, proudly carrying the Stars and Stripes.

During the afternoon, crowds packed St John's churchyard for another thanksgiving service preceded by a parade of over 700 young people representing the town's youth organisations, who marched to the church from the South Street car park.

Once again, the evening was turned over to dancing, but on this occasion, it was at the floodlit Huish ground where a huge crowd danced to Bill Kelly's Band. There was a concert in the Sidney Gardens given by the Westland Male Voice Choir and the Salvation Army band played in the Borough.

However, the highlight of the evening (quite literally) was the huge bonfire built on the top of Summerhouse Hill. At 10 p.m. precisely, the bonfire was lit by column officer Charles Mitchell of the national fire service, and as the flames roared up, they took with them a more-than-life-size effigy of Adolf Hitler while adults and children danced a round the blaze.

For two days across the nation, people danced, sang, and thoroughly enjoyed themselves, forgetting, perhaps, for a short time, the savage war still to be fought to a conclusion in the Far East, and the shortages and rationing that would continue for a long time to come.

Some of the happiest events in the town were the many children's street parties when the years of shortages and rationing were forgotten for a day. 'I've never seen so many happy faces in my life,' exclaimed Yeovil's mayor, as he concluded his visits to children's street parties across the town in the days following VE-Day on 8 May 1945; how right he was. The years of shortages and rationing were forgotten as the youngsters enjoyed the freely given food and soft drinks in quantities, which many had never previously experienced.

On 9 May, Park Street held two parties, one at each end. An organiser told the *Western Gazette* that 'I had a bomb dropped behind my back door and out of nine dropped, ours was the one which did not explode. We were lucky and I felt I must do something for the children'. Twenty children were entertained in Bond Street for which Mr Chubb, baker and confectioner, supplied an iced cake. In South Street from Bond Street to

Penn Hill, twelve youngsters were given a party and twenty children in Woodland Grove sat down to a splendid tea.

During the days that followed, Yeovil got into a party mood, and all across the town, children from toddlers to teenagers enjoyed tea and entertainment. In some streets, people brought out radios and gramophones, while others played accordions or pianos.

The *Western Gazette* reporters were out and about at the parties and recorded their impressions. At Glenville Road, about forty children were entertained and local tradesmen supplied oranges and other goodies, with ice cream served from a butcher's refrigerator. The party was followed by singing, races, and games.

One of the largest parties was at Wellington Street, where eighty-five youngsters sat down to a tea supplied by parents and local shopkeepers; one of the town's wholesalers provided a crate of oranges. Each child was given a sixpenny savings stamp.

At Hillcrest Road, three parties were given and a feature of one party was a large iced VE-cake decorated with the flags of the allies. Following comic sketches by Mr Way and Mr Tompkins, an effigy of Hitler was burnt.

In Westfield Crescent, the children's tea was followed by a mothers' tea and games. Nearby in Westfield Avenue and Westfield Place, there was tea and ice creams followed by sports. Each of the youngsters received a silver threepenny piece and an orange. The young people of Stiby Road enjoyed games and music led by Mr Gerrard at the Westfield Hotel and sat down to tea in the skittle alley.

At the other side of Yeovil, on Eastland Road, over 100 children were entertained outside the Nelson Inn and each youngster was given an orange and a shilling.

Park Street held a third party with a miniature sports meeting and Mr Scanes provided the amusement dressed up as the popular stage and film character 'Old Mother Riley'.

Ninety-four children partook of tea, fancy cakes and oranges on the Yeovil girls high school playing field, and Mr Fickus entertained the youngsters with songs and dance music. Later, parents joined in the dancing.

Two ladies—one of whose husbands was missing presumed killed and the other whose son had been killed in the army—organised a party for over forty children in the playground of the Westfield Baptist church to which all their parents were invited. Oranges and ice cream were top of the menu.

Westfield Road children had a three-tier iced VE-cake decorated with Union Jacks, and enjoyed ices, chocolate bars, sweets, oranges, and mineral waters followed by sports and games.

There was much excitement at the Eastville party when—after enjoying a sumptuous tea, community singing, games, and races—a bonfire was lit, fireworks were let off, and the fire brigade arrived. It transpired that 'a well-intentioned person' seeing the blaze thought that one of the nearby glove factories was on fire and called the brigade.

Southville's party was not so dramatic but after tea there was community singing and dancing through to midnight. Mr Roy Parsons, a former prisoner of war, presented each child with a sixpenny piece.

The *Western Gazette* reported:

On Thursday, a party was given for the children of the lower half of Marclose. Pte. Tucker, a repatriated prisoner of war was present. On Friday, there were sports for the children (postponed from the previous night). The party included Flight Sgt D. Warr and Trooper L.F. Rendell, returned prisoners of war. On Saturday night the residents held a sing-song and dance in honour of the return after three and a half years as a prisoner of war of Trooper Rendell to whom they presented a wallet and a savings certificate.

Rain forced the Percy and Alexandra Roads' party to adjourn to St Michael's Hall where Mr E Robbins' forty-year-old 'Bicycle Made for Two' provided much merriment, especially when the mayoress tried to ride it. During the evening, the rain cleared up and the dancing in Percy Road went on until midnight. Some rockets supplied by Mr Robbins were fired off to enliven the proceedings.

Eighty youngsters sat down to tea in Messrs Palmer and Snell's yard organised by Mrs Cousins of the Pall hotel. There were two large iced cakes, entertainment by Marco Lavonte and music from the Bill Kelly Band.

Many other parties were held in Yeovil, which sadly went unrecorded, except perhaps, in the memories of those who enjoyed them.

VJ-Day

On Friday 17 August 1945, the *Western Gazette* reported the announcement on midnight on Tuesday the 14th of the surrender of Japan:

[It] caught the majority of people in the South and West unprepared for the immediate celebration of the end of the war. Comparatively few of the thousands of people who, for days, had so anxiously awaited the great news heard the Prime Minister Mr. C. R. Attlee give the signal to all to 'relax and enjoy themselves in the knowledge of work well done'. Only in towns where social life is continued till a later hour was there immediate reaction to the relief which the announcement brought and quickly there were scenes of spontaneous rejoicing in the streets and in private houses. The majority of people were unaware of the return of peace until the first of the V.J.-days was fairly well advanced. Then the preparations of local authorities and householders were accelerated and soon scenes reminiscent of V.E.-day were markedly in evidence. Throughout the South and West, the celebrations were on much of the same scale and form as on the earlier occasion - thanksgiving services, ceremonial parades and music in the daytime, with the climax of fireworks, bonfires, the floodlighting of historic and public buildings, and dancing and unrestrained merrymaking in brilliantly lit streets and squares.

Amid all the rejoicings there was grateful remembrance of the glorious part which the Hampshire, Dorset, Somerset and Wiltshire Regiments had played in the defeat of the enemy.

Though there were remarkable scenes of joy and thanksgiving in Yeovil, there was no repetition of the wild hilarity which marked the end of the European war. Many workers who had not heard the radio announcements started out for work as usual. Townspeople were early astir, and hurriedly put out flags, bunting and streamers. Housewives formed long queues for food, but the longest queue was in Middle Street for fireworks.

The Mayor and Corporation attended a thanksgiving service conducted by the Vicar of Yeovil (Preb. H. Mortlock Treen), at the Parish Church and the service was relayed to a gathering outside. The bells rang out their joyous peals throughout the day.

Over 8,000 assembled in the Borough on Wednesday evening and were addressed by the Mayor (Mr. W.S. Vosper), who asked them to remember with reverence and pride those who had fallen—both Servicemen and civilians—and those who had been maimed or wounded or were prisoners. He paid tribute to the work of the Forces and Civil Defence, and other services, and expressed the fervent hope that all would now be allowed to devote their thoughts and energies to the creation of a structure in which all people will live in real peace, happiness and prosperity.

Public houses which had been granted an extension until midnight were forced to close their doors considerably earlier through lack of supplies. In some cases, 'Sold out' notices appeared before 10 o'clock.

The Salvation Army gave a performance in Bide's Garden in the evening.

Bill Kelly's Band provided music in the Borough, and there were boisterous scenes as the night wore on. Hundreds of people were singing, shouting and dancing. Floodlights blazed down until well after midnight and crackers, rockets and thunderflashes provided a constant succession of bangs and explosions. Two or three children had eye injuries—fortunately not serious—as a result of explosions. The beautiful old church stood floodlit in all its grandeur, and provided welcome solitude and peace only a few yards away from the dancing and singing crowds. There were also illuminations in Bide's Garden.

An emergency centre manned by women members of the ladies' V.A.D. under Commandant Miss K. Marsh, at the Police Station dealt with a number of cases of fainting, and ambulances had several times to make their way through the crowd. Music came to an impromptu end at 11.40 p.m. when the wires from the microphone to the loudspeakers around the Borough were torn away but the crowd did not disperse until nearly three. An impromptu 'band' played request items from the bandstand. A bonfire on the Mudford Road Playing Fields could be seen for miles around.

All throughout the next day, the bells of St John's Church rang out, and in the evening, crowds again filled the Borough, singing and dancing till late. The pubs ran out of beer and cider, so they had to close early.

The town's children enjoyed parties during the days that followed, and out came the hoarded goodies to give them a time to remember. The author retains a very fond memory of the Orchard Street party held on the back lawn of his home at number 37.

We had tea and games, and the huge iced cake was cut by our guest of honour and neighbour, Cpl Horace Clarke, RAF, back from service in North Africa. Lighting and music were supplied by Mr Wooton of Richmond Road, and after dark we had fireworks.

Twenty-seven children from the top of St Michael's Avenue were entertained to a tea and film show in a marquee, followed in the evening by singing, dancing, and a bonfire with fireworks.

On the afternoon of Saturday 8 September, a tea party was given to over 100 children from the Highfield and Hillcrest Road area, followed by a fancy-dress parade, sports, dancing, and a treasure hunt rounded off by fireworks. The Wesleyan chapel in Great Western Terrace was the venue for a tea and entertainment for local youngsters with parents and friends dancing up to midnight in St Michael's Avenue. The residents of Eliotts Drive, Albert Close, and Barnet Close really pushed the boat out with a celebration day on 8 September. There was a fancy-dress parade, baby show, victory tea, and children's sports, followed by dancing in the road until midnight.

The children of the Wraxhill Road area held their victory celebration in the recently built St Mary's hall, and the *Western Gazette* reported:

> The Mayor (Mr. W.S. Vosper), accompanied by the Mayoress opened the proceedings. A delightful touch was given to the opening ceremony by the presentation of a bouquet to the Mayoress by little Catherine Horwood, the infant daughter of Yeovil's V.C. [Lt. Alec Horwood VC, DCM.]

Even the most enjoyable celebrations can have their reckoning, and at the meeting of the town council on 10 September, it was reported that the VE and VJ celebrations had cost the ratepayers £400, which would be met from a supplementary rate.

In September 1945

There was also a slightly darker side of the VJ-Day celebrations when some three weeks later in September, the Wes*tern Gazette* reported that during the day, a large number of 'thunder-flashes' had been let off. Thunder-flashes were large military fireworks mainly used to simulate explosions on the battlefield but without the resulting injuries (although if one went off close beside you it could be quite alarming as the author recalled from personal experience some years before in HM's armed forces). The *Gazette* stated that there a been a number of incidents involving youngsters throwing fireworks and thunder-flashes about the streets, and girls being chased through the town by boys throwing fireworks at them and burning their clothing. More worrying, in the newspaper's opinion, were suggestions that adults were also involved in such incidents:

> One occurrence which might have resulted in a serious fire took place recently when a lighted firework was put through a letter box of a house catching alight a mat just inside the door and considerably alarming the occupants.

The residents of Preston Grove and Road were also up in arms about the nuisance being caused by soldiers in high spirits returning to Houndstone and Lufton camps at night. Gates were taken off their hinges, garbage from refuse bins tipped over gardens, and the bins and their lids thrown about in the roads. Included in the list of transgressions was the damage to streetlights, and the borough council and the police were being pressed to take steps to stop these nuisances.

Early in September 1945, a new system was introduced to call out part-time firemen for emergency duty. Between the hours of 6 a.m. and 10 p.m., a steady continuous note would be sounded for one minute by the air-raid siren on the police station. The siren would continue to be used for many years as the part-timers' call-out.

One emergency to which the firemen were not called happened on Tuesday 18 September, when a bullock broke away from a herd being driven up Silver Street from the market. Then followed a six-hour chase by pedestrians and policemen on bicycles during which two people were gored before the bullock was cornered and shot dead by a slaughter man in a back garden in Mary Street. The bullock had escaped at about 3 p.m. and charged straight at PC Sams, who was on traffic point duty in the Borough. Unable to avoid the beast, the officer was bowled over and received injuries to his neck and head. An ambulance was called, and the constable was taken to hospital from which he was discharged after treatment. Meanwhile, the bullock rampaged around the town centre until it was cornered at Penn Hill. However, the wily beast broke out through a loosely secured gate, narrowly missing several police officers and spectators, and continued to charge about the town. Finally, the bullock was brought to bay in Mary Street but not before it had attacked Mr Trent of number 13, goring his leg. This time, there would be no escape, and the animal was shot.

By coincidence, Tuesday 18 September was the day on which a new Austin 24 army type ambulance was delivered to the Yeovil detachment of Somerset/19 VAD at their station in Salthouse Lane.

Gainsborough Film Studio's 'new film star', Michael Rennie, was at the Gaumont cinema on the evening of Friday 7 September, to judge the divisional final of the old-time song contest held in connection with the film *I'll be Your Sweetheart*, in which he took the lead role. Earlier in the day, the star had visited Aplin and Barrett's dairy produce factory in Newton Road, and seeing glove-making at Messrs Whitby Bros' factory off Middle Street.

Local soprano Sylvia Rowlands appeared in the BBC's 'All Star' variety programme on 17 September.

Finally, at 9.30 on Sunday morning, 9 September 1945, three buses left Orchard Street on the street's Victory Outing and drove to West Bay. There followed a lunch stop on the top of Abbotsbury Hill at noon, and the outing departed at a quarter to one to spend the afternoon at Weymouth—a very enjoyable day was had by all.

The First Post-war Christmas, 1945

During the weeks leading up to the first post-war Christmas, the weather was very wet, there were heavy thunderstorms and severe gales across the West Country, but Christmas Day was 'green and almost spring-like'.

The *Western Gazette* reported the following happening in Yeovil:

Christmas was the mildest and quietest for six years. There were bright periods of sunshine on Christmas Day and unusual floral decorations in many houses indicated the mildness of the season. Mr. E.C. Fox, of Swallowcliffe Gardens, picked sprays of cherry blossom from a tree flowering in the open and many residents had a selection of flowers rarely seen in gardens at this period of the year.

Even though the war was over, the strict rationing of food, clothing, and other essentials continued and combined to result in what could only be described as an austerity Christmas.

However, it was Christmas, and we were finally at peace. On Christmas Eve, the shops were lit up, the pubs were full, and people flocked into the town to enjoy the atmosphere, the first truly festive season since 1938. The safe return of fathers, sons, and daughters from the war added to families' Christmas cheer.

One soldier who would not be at home was Regimental Sergeant Major F. McCrombie, serving with the Royal Army Ordnance Corps in Nairobi, Kenya, but who managed to make a long-distance telephone Christmas greeting to his wife, Caroline, who was living at 89 Goldcroft. Mrs McCrombie told a *Western Gazette* reporter that 'Although so many hundreds of miles away, I could hear him clearly and could recognise his voice'.

On Friday and Saturday 21 and 22 December, special trains left the Town and Pen Mill stations carrying over 2,000 personnel from Houndstone and Lufton camps and RNAS Yeovilton home for Christmas leave, and on Thursday the 27th, five special trains brought them back.

Carols were sung on Christmas Eve in the streets by various church and chapel choirs, and on three nights during the week before Christmas, youngsters from Huish Junior school together with their teachers, sang carols in Huish and in the Westfield area collecting £11 17s 9d, of which £5 was sent to the Yeovil hospital fund and the balance to the school fund.

On Friday 22 December, the mayor and mayoress carried out the traditional visits to the Preston Close public assistance institution, the alms-houses, and the district hospital to wish everyone a happy Christmas.

The one baby born in the maternity home by the Five Cross Roads on Christmas Day, a was a boy for Mr and Mrs Allen of Glenthorne Avenue. The fathers of the eight babies remaining in the home over Christmas were invited to tea and supper with their wives and new offspring. As well as entertaining the families, the mothers received presents of cushions made from blackout material and sponge bags made 'from odds and ends' by the matron and her nursing staff; the babies received dolls and teddy bears. The simple gifts to the mothers reflected the shortage of everyday material goods.

In the district hospital, there was turkey and plum puddings for the patients' Christmas Dinner and in the afternoon, visiting relatives and friends were entertained to tea. Each patient received a gift from the hospital Christmas fund, face powder, and writing paper for the women, toys for the children, and shaving soap and cigarettes for the men. The nursing staff gave a concert in the men's ward on Christmas evening and on Boxing evening in the women's ward.

At the public assistance institution, the *Western Gazette* reported that 'Christmas fare did not run to poultry. There were 118 inmates, and pork and plum puddings were enjoyed.'

Yeovil's head postmaster played tribute to the teamwork of his staff and the eighty-six extra part-time postmen, the majority of whom were senior boys at Yeovil School, and he especially praised members of the public for posting early, which had enabled all letters received on Christmas morning to be delivered that day. He went on to say that letter traffic was 11 per cent up on Christmas 1944—341,286 letters went through the franking machines from 13 to 24 December. However, compared with 1944, there was a decrease in the number of telephone calls and telegrams.

The *Gazette* reported that 'A two-day meeting under the National Hunt rules at Wincanton began on Boxing Day. There was a festive air of Christmas holidays among the large crowd present in spite of continuing austerity'. The *Western Gazette's* sentiment just about sums up Christmas 1945.

Around the Town in 1945

Home from the Faroes
In January, Gunner Nat Biggin, of the Half Moon hotel, Silver Street, was home on leave from the Danish Faroe Islands, which lie between the Orkneys and Iceland; he told the *Western Gazette* that this was his first glimpse of Yeovil for some years. He went on to say that because of the severe Arctic conditions in these remote islands, this was one of the few overseas stations where leave was made compulsory and troops were sent at intervals to recuperate in Scotland.

'The men in the Faroes do not share in the headlines like those on the battle fronts but one day,' said Gunner Biggins, 'an equally interesting story will be told'.

The 'All-Electric Post-War Kitchen'
During March, an 'all-electric post-war kitchen' was on display in Yeovil at the Wessex Electricity Company's Princes Street showrooms made up of units that could be rearranged and purchased separately. On 9 March, the *Western Gazette* described the 'kitchen of the future':

The sink has an electric storage heater providing enough hot water for general household use, an electrically operated clothes washer and power-driven wringer, a drying cupboard containing racks and shelves for wet clothes, towels and general laundry. Streamlined model cooker of the latest post-war design, refrigerator with automatic temperature control, tubular fluorescent lighting without shadow or glare, low temperature panel heaters, switch sockets connecting the accessories-kettle, toaster, mixer, iron &c. An electric clock is mounted on a corner cupboard, and a cooking time signal can be added when these are available. There is a book shelf for cookery and reference books, a recessed cupboard with a mirror panelled door to hold toilet requisites and first aid outfit, a small radio receiver and a tradesmen's serving hatch. There is also shown an all-electric bath-room.

Late for Work

During the war, you could be prosecuted for being persistently late for work and the authorities took a dim view of this threat to production. During the week before VE-Day in May, a girl was fined £2, with the option of a month in prison for non-payment, following her plea of guilty to being persistently late for work at Westland Aircraft between November 1944 and January 1945. The bench was told that in forty-six days, the girl had only been punctual on two days and her lateness amounted to thirty-three hours and thirty-three minutes. In her defence, the girl stated that she had been unwell and had also stayed at home to look after her married sister who could not get help during her confinement.

A Deadly Swap

In March, a thirteen-year-old boy admitted to the county juvenile court that he had climbed onto a United States Army lorry, opened a weapons box, removed a Thompson sub-machine gun, and had taken it home. A few days later, he swapped it with another lad for a 0.22 pistol and the court was told by this youngster that he had found the pistol on the floor of his school changing room. He had thought that both the pistol and the sub-machine gun were toys. The court heard that the two boys had no ammunition for either weapon, and that the Thompson had only been taken to 'muck about with'. Putting the thirteen-year-old on a year's probation, the chairman suggested that he join a youth organisation.

Queues

A resident of Glenthorne Avenue's letter to the editor of the *Western Gazette* was published on 9 November:

> Sir, Referring to the recent comments which from time to time have appeared in your paper regarding the queuing in Yeovil, which still appears to be as bad as ever, during the past few weeks I have had to take a hand with the shopping. I have formed the opinion that all the culprits are some shop keepers. All shops should have a recognised and official opening time, just as they have a compulsory closing time. I have discovered that certain shops will not open their doors until a queue has formed outside their shops. On one occasion, I went into a confectioner's shop whose door was wide open and the window full of cakes. Although the time was 9.45 a.m. and no doubt the door had been left open by mistake. I was told to wait outside as the shop was not yet open for trade. Of course I did. Then again, I tried for biscuits at a multiple shop, where ample were offered for sale by a little girl hardly tall enough to look over the counter. Here again I was told that I must wait as they hadn't started to sell. On another occasion I tried for apples at a fruit shop, only to be told that there was no room for serving in the shop; would I mind waiting outside on the pavement—in other words would I start a queue for a cheap advertisement. I am convinced that if such shops were compelled to open in the morning at a fixed and reasonable hour just as they are compelled to close at night, it would help considerably towards reducing queues.

A Lucky Escape

Just before Christmas, a Royal Army Service Corps despatch rider had a lucky escape from injury when his motorcycle exploded in flames as he started it in Middle Street. Pte McCleas managed to throw himself clear as the flames erupted. Within minutes, the fire brigade was on the scene and extinguished the blaze.

A German POW Injured

In early December, Carlos Spartaro (a German POW working in the Electric Saw Mills at Sparkford) was admitted to Yeovil hospital suffering from head injuries resulting from a violent blow as he helped with handling a timber winch. There was no report on the outcome.

Bananas

During the last week of December, 600 bunches of bananas were ripening in Messrs T. Mansfield and Co's Sherborne Road warehouse, but the *Western Gazette* reported that they were not for Yeovilians because when they were ready they would be sent to Taunton as there were no ripening facilities in the county town. Yeovil would have to wait until the end of January for its supply. An employee of Messrs Mansfield told the *Gazette* that many of the townsfolk who had visited the warehouse had not seen a banana for six years and quite a few of the youngsters had never seen one.

10

Remembrance

The War Memorials

Yeovil has two public war memorials, one in the Borough and the second at Preston Plucknett.

The Borough

The war memorial in the Borough remembers the men, women, and children from the town who lost their lives in the First and Second World Wars and the Falklands Conflict of 1982. In 2018, the memorial was renovated, with the bronze plaques replaced with new ones by the Yeovil town council.

The following men from the three services represent those who fought in the Second World War from 1939–45, and who are remembered on the Borough memorial.

The Royal Navy

Petty Officer John Perry, RN

Petty Officer Perry was a member of the ship's company of HMS *River Tyne*, a former merchant steamer sent with two other old merchant ships commandeered by the Royal Navy and renamed, HMS *Kaupo* and HMS *Jacobus,* to block Dieppe harbour, as the German Army swept west during the invasion of France in June 1940. The top-secret operation involved the ships being sunk at the entrance to the harbour, thus denying its use to the Germans as a naval base and port for the feared invasion of the United Kingdom.

The three block ships, escorted by the destroyer HMS *Vega* and several motor torpedo boats left Portsmouth early on Sunday 9 June, arriving off Dieppe at 4 o'clock the following morning. Despite the strong tidal currents, the *Kaupo* and the *Jacobus* were anchored at the harbour entrance, the scuttling charges blown, and the two ships settled on the seabed and sealed the port.

However, as the *River Tyne* was being manoeuvred into position, she struck a mine that exploded towards the stern, broke the propeller shaft, wrecked the main engine, and ripped out vital steam pipes. The ship stopped dead in the water, her back broken and with all communications to the rear carried away in the blast. The *River Tyne* began to drift from the entrance, but the efforts to let go the port bow anchor and the stern anchor failed as Petty Officer Ricketts (charged with releasing the forward anchor) was badly injured in the explosion and Petty Officer John Perry (in charge at the stern) was killed and his team of three ratings knocked unconscious with head wounds.

The order was given to abandon ship, the crew taken off by a motor torpedo boat, the charges were blown, and HMS *River Tyne* sank some 500 m from the entrance to Dieppe harbour.

Petty Officer John Perry had served for twenty-three years in the Royal Navy and on returning to civilian life had been employed at Westland Aircraft. He left a widow, a son, and a daughter, at home in Westland Road, and tragically, he was the only fatal casualty in the operation.

Leading Wireman Arthur Ball, RN

Twenty-year-old leading wireman (electrician) Arthur Ball was a member of the crew of HM landing craft gun (medium) *102*, and on 1 November 1944, British commandoes and British and Canadian infantry were landed on the island of Walcheren in an operation to clear the Germans from the approaches to the port of Antwerp and thereby open its essential dock facilities.

HM landing craft gun (medium) *102*, with a crew of three officers and thirty men and armed with two 25-pounder guns and eight machine guns, in company with HM landing craft (medium) *101*, were part of the fire support for the landing. The landing craft *102* ran in under heavy fire, beached, and opened fire on an enemy strong point, but in turn was subjected to overwhelming enemy fire and totally destroyed; there were no survivors. In turn, landing craft 101 was sunk by heavy enemy fire but her crew escaped with few casualties.

The Army

Major Sydney C. W. Young, MC

The 7th Bn Somerset Light Infantry, was part of the 43rd Wessex Division, 30 Corps, was in the advance to join up with the airborne forces battling at Arnhem, and on Saturday, 23 September 1944, the battalion was in the vicinity of the village of Oosterhout. Major Young was leading 'D' Company when they were pinned down by German infantry supported by a tank on the southern fringes of the village, and it was during a reconnaissance of enemy positions that he was mortally wounded.

Just a fortnight later, on 6 October, the *Western Gazette* reported:

Following an announcement that her husband, Major Sydney C.W. Young, Somerset Light Infantry, had been granted an immediate award of the Military Cross, Mrs. Young of Oxen Close, 186 Ilchester Road, received the sad news that he had died of wounds in September.

The Military Cross citation stated:

Major S.C.W. Young, 7 Som. LI. On 2nd July 1944 at Tourville, this officer led a composite battle patrol of infantry carriers, A/Tk guns and 3in. mortars to obtain information on enemy dispositions in Verson and Jumeaux. Throughout the operation he showed great initiative and skill in handling the force under his command and penetrating 3 miles into enemy territory obtained valuable information of concealed enemy M.G. and Mortar emplacements which had been harassing our own. In addition to wounding or killing six of the enemy, the patrol was able to give information which subsequently enabled our troops to be more suitably disposed for a forthcoming major operation. Throughout the operation his confidence and personal bravery inspired the men in accomplishing a bold venture with outstanding success.

Private Ernest William Timbrell

Pte Ernest Timbrell, serving with the 1st Bn The Parachute Regiment, was reported missing during the battle at Arnhem in September 1944; subsequently, it was announced in a German broadcast that he had been killed during the second day of the battle on 18 September as the battalion fought to secure the Arnhem bridge. He was the youngest son of Mr and Mrs Timbrell of 1 Westfield Place, leaving a widow and a three-year-old son. Before being called up, he had been employed by the Royal London Insurance Co.

The Royal Air Force

Corporal Bernard Nowell, RAF

Corporal Nowell, serving with 15 Group Coastal Command detachment at RAF Mount Batten, Plymouth, was a crewman on board a Walrus of No. 10 Squadron, Royal Australian Air Force. The aircraft left Mount Batten at 3 a.m. on 18 June 1940 and crashed at Ploudaniel, a village about 21 km north-east of Brest, with the loss of all four personnel— pilot, Flt Lt J. N. Bell, RAAF; air observer, Sgt C. W. Harris, RAAF; crew, Cpl B. F. Nowell, RAF; and Captain N. E. Hope, Intelligence Corps. No. 10 Squadron was carrying out maritime reconnaissance duties and flying VIPs to France during the last days of the German invasion, and also to Malta.

The occupants of the Walrus were on a top-secret mission. Captain Hope—who had travelled widely before the outbreak of the Second World War and spoke fluent French and Spanish—was attached to Section 'D' of the Secret Intelligence Service (MI6) and was on a mission directly ordered by the prime minister, Winston Churchill, to rescue the wife and daughter of General Charles de Gaulle from Brittany in France. The aircraft was heading for Carantec on the Brittany coast, and at about 4 a.m., the Walrus crashed near the village of Ploudaniel. The cause of the crash was never properly established, but two possible reasons have been put forward. One report stated that a radio transmission from the aircraft indicated that it was being attacked by enemy aircraft, and the second from local villagers, was that the Walrus had been brought down by a German anti-aircraft battery at Valeury as it crossed the coast. Whatever the cause, the aircraft was some thirty-five kilometres off course to the west of the planned route when it crashed.

Sergeant A. T. Barlow, RAFVR

Sergeant Arnold Barlow, whose parents lived at 48 St Michael's Avenue, joined the RAF in 1941. During the night of 24–25 June 1943, he was the second navigator on Lancaster ED858 GT-R flying on his fourteenth operation with 156 Squadron, Bomber Command, a target marking pathfinder squadron, and one of 650 bombers attacking Elberfeld, a suburb of Wuppertal in the German Ruhr. Arnold was killed when his Lancaster was shot down and crashed near Cologne—one of two that the squadron lost on the raid.

The Prisoners of War

Lance Corporal P. H. Perry

Philip Perry enlisted in the Army from his home in Matthews Road in December 1939 as a storeman in the Royal Army Ordnance Corps and served with BEF, being evacuated back to England from France on 12 June 1940. In November 1941, he was serving in Iraq with the 86th Anti-tank Regiment, Royal Artillery, and was posted to Singapore. On its surrender to the Japanese in February 1942, Philip became a prisoner of war and died from colitis in a Malayan prison camp on 23 May 1943.

Flight Sergeant Leslie Chant, RAFVR

FS Chant was a bomb aimer flying in Halifax bombers operated by No. 35 Squadron, Bomber Command, a pathfinder squadron, based at RAF Station Gravely, Cambridgeshire, and on the night of 20 February 1944, the squadron participated in a raid on the German city of Leipzig. FS Chant, on his forty-eighth mission, was a member of the crew of Halifax LV864, which became airborne at 12.05 a.m., but was shot down in flames by a German night fighter. Four of the seven crew members bailed out from heights ranging from 6000 feet to less than 900 feet, and FS Chant was one of the survivors. He was taken prisoner and interned in *Stalag* 357 at Oerbke, near Fallingbostel, Germany, but sadly died at the camp of a coronary attack on 2 December 1944.

FS Chant had volunteered for the RAF in 1941 and had received his aircrew training in Canada. During his operational tours with Bomber Command he had taken part in raids on Berlin, Munich, and other German targets.

Prior to joining the RAF, Leslie Chant had been a popular staff member of the Yeovil borough council.

Preston Plucknett

Until the boundaries of the borough of Yeovil were extended westward in 1929, Preston Plucknett was a separate parish and in 1920 a war memorial was dedicated to the men of the village who died in the First World War and now bears the names of two local men who died between 1939 and 1945.

Driver Charles Mark Old

Charles Old was a driver serving with the Royal Army Service Corps when he was killed on 13 October 1945, the war had been over two months. The *Western Gazette* reported his death on 26 October:

> News was received on Tuesday October 16th, of the death of Charles Mark Old, the third son of Mr. Edwin Old of the Bakery, (Preston Plucknett), in an air crash over Belgium. The 'plane was on its way to the Middle East. He had lived all his life in Preston before entering the Army. He was educated at the Preston Church School and sang as a boy in the church choir. On leaving school he entered his father's business. He was married in 1942 to Olive Pitfield of Whitchurch, Dorset.

The twenty-five-year-old Charles lies at peace in Brussels town cemetery.

Lance Corporal Thomas Henry Steel

Twenty-two-year-old L/Cpl Thomas Steel of the 1st Bn Grenadier Guards had been stationed in Yeovil at the outbreak of the Second World War where he met Iris, his future wife. Posted to France, he was evacuated from Dunkirk with the BEF having suffered shrapnel wounds, and returning to Yeovil, married Iris on 10 June 1940. When serving with the Grenadier Guards at Piddlehinton Camp in Dorset, he was killed in a traffic accident while driving a military vehicle on duty. Thomas lies in Yeovil Cemetery.